TED
TALKS

The Official TED Guide
to Public Speaking

TED
TALKS

The **Official TED Guide** to Public Speaking

CHRIS ANDERSON

headline

First published in Great Britain in 2016
by HEADLINE PUBLISHING GROUP

1

Cataloguing in Publication Data is available from the British Library

Hardback ISBN 978 1 4722 2804 8
Trade Paperback ISBN 978 1 4722 2805 5

Printed and bound by CPI Group (UK) Ltd, Croydon CR0 4YY

HEADLINE PUBLISHING GROUP
An Hachette UK Company
Carmelite House
50 Victoria Embankment
London EC4Y 0DZ

www.headline.co.uk
www.hachette.co.uk

Inspired by Zoe Anderson (1986–2010).

Life is fleeting. Ideas, inspiration, and love endure.

CONTENTS

Prologue: The New Age of Fire   ix

FOUNDATION

1. PRESENTATION LITERACY: The Skill You Can Build   3
2. IDEA BUILDING: The Gift in Every Great Talk   11
3. COMMON TRAPS: Four Talk Styles to Avoid   22
4. THE THROUGHLINE: What's Your Point?   30

TALK TOOLS

5. CONNECTION: Get Personal   47
6. NARRATION: The Irresistible Allure of Stories   63
7. EXPLANATION: How to Explain Tough Concepts   72
8. PERSUASION: Reason Can Change Minds Forever   86
9. REVELATION: Take My Breath Away!   97

PREPARATION PROCESS

10. VISUALS: Those Slides Hurt!   113
11. SCRIPTING: To Memorize or Not to Memorize?   130
12. RUN-THROUGHS: Wait, I Need to Rehearse?   148
13. OPEN AND CLOSE: What Kind of Impression
    Would You Like to Make?   156

ON STAGE

14. WARDROBE: What Should I Wear?   179

15. MENTAL PREP: How Do I Control My Nerves?   183

16. SETUP: Lectern, Confidence Monitor, Note Cards,
or (Gulp) Nothing?   189

17. VOICE AND PRESENCE: Give Your Words
the Life They Deserve   198

18. FORMAT INNOVATION: The Promise
(and Peril) of Full-Spectrum Talks   209

REFLECTION

19. TALK RENAISSANCE: The Interconnectedness of Knowledge   227

20. WHY THIS MATTERS: The Interconnectedness of People   238

21. YOUR TURN: The Philosopher's Secret   247

Acknowledgments   253

Appendix: Talks Referenced within the Book   255

Index   259

THE NEW AGE OF FIRE

The house lights dim. A woman, her palms sweating, her legs trembling just a little, steps out onto the stage. A spotlight hits her face, and 1,200 pairs of eyes lock onto hers. The audience senses her nervousness. There is palpable tension in the room. She clears her throat and starts to speak.

What happens next is astounding.

The 1,200 brains inside the heads of 1,200 independent individuals start to behave very strangely. They begin to sync up. A magic spell woven by the woman washes over each person. They gasp together. Laugh together. Weep together. And as they do so, something else happens. Rich, neurologically encoded patterns of information inside the woman's brain are somehow copied and transferred to the 1,200 brains in the audience. These patterns will remain in those brains for the rest of their lives, potentially impacting their behavior years into the future.

The woman on the stage is weaving wonder, not witchcraft. But her skills are as potent as any sorcery.

Ants shape each other's behavior by exchanging chemicals. We do it by standing in front of each other, peering into each other's eyes, waving our hands and emitting strange sounds from our mouths. Human-to-human communication is a true wonder of the world. We do it unconsciously every day. And it reaches its most intense form on the public stage.

The purpose of this book is to explain how the miracle of powerful public speaking is achieved, and to equip you to give it your best shot. But one thing needs emphasizing right at the start.

There is no one way to give a great talk. The world of knowledge is far too big and the range of speakers and of audiences and of talk settings is far too varied for that. Any attempt to apply a single set formula is likely to backfire. Audiences see through it in an instant and feel manipulated.

Indeed, even if there were a successful formula at one moment in time, it wouldn't stay successful for long. That's because a key part of the appeal of a great talk is its freshness. We're humans. We don't like same old, same old. If your talk feels too similar to a talk someone has already heard, it is bound to have less impact. The last thing we want is for everyone to sound the same or for anyone to sound as though he's faking it.

So you should not think of the advice in this book as *rules* prescribing a single way to speak. Instead think of it as offering you a set of *tools* designed to encourage variety. Just use the ones that are right for you and for the speaking opportunity you're facing. Your only real job in giving a talk is to have something valuable to say, and to say it authentically in your own unique way.

You may find it more natural than you think. Public speaking is an ancient art, wired deeply into our minds. Archaeological discoveries dating back hundreds of thousands of years have found community meeting sites where our ancestors gathered around fire. In every culture on earth, as language developed, people learned to share their stories, hopes, and dreams.

Imagine a typical scene. It is after nightfall. The campfire is ablaze. The logs crackle and spit under a starry sky. An elder rises, and all eyes turn and lock onto the wise, wrinkled face, illuminated by the flickering light. The story begins. And as the storyteller speaks, each listener imagines the events that are being described. That imagination brings with it the same emotions shared by the characters in the story. This is a profoundly powerful process. It is the literal alignment of multiple minds into a shared consciousness. For a period of time, the campfire participants act as if they were a single life form. They may rise together, dance together, chant together. From this shared backdrop, it is a short step to the desire to act together, to decide to embark together on a journey, a battle, a building, a celebration.

The same is true today. As a leader — or as an advocate — public speaking is the key to unlocking empathy, stirring excitement, sharing knowledge and insights, and promoting a shared dream.

Indeed, the spoken word has actually gained new powers. Our campfire is now the whole world. Thanks to the Internet, a single talk in a single theater can end up being seen by millions of people. Just as the printing press massively amplified the power of authors, so the web is massively amplifying the impact of speakers. It is allowing anyone anywhere with online access (and within a decade or so, we can expect almost every village on earth to be connected) to summon the world's greatest teachers to their homes and learn from them directly. Suddenly an ancient art has global reach.

This revolution has sparked a renaissance in public speaking. Many of us have suffered years of long, boring lectures at university; interminable sermons at church; or roll-your-eyes predictable political stump speeches. It doesn't have to be that way.

Done right, a talk can electrify a room and transform an audience's worldview. Done right, a talk is more powerful than anything in written form. Writing gives us the words. Speaking brings with it a whole new toolbox. When we peer into a speaker's eyes; listen to the tone of her voice; sense her vulnerability, her intelligence, her passion, we are tapping into unconscious skills that have been fine-tuned over hundreds of thousands of years. Skills that can galvanize, empower, inspire.

What is more, we can enhance these skills in ways the ancients could never have imagined: The ability to show — right there in beautiful high-resolution — any image that a human can photograph or imagine. The ability to weave in video and music. The ability to draw on research tools that present the entire body of human knowledge to anyone in reach of a smartphone.

The good news is, these skills are teachable. They absolutely are. And that means that there's a new superpower that anyone, young or old, can benefit from. It's called *presentation literacy*. We live in an era where the best way to make a dent on the world may no longer be to write a letter to the editor or publish a book. It may be simply to stand up and say something . . . because both the words and the passion with which they are delivered can now spread across the world at warp speed.

In the twenty-first century, presentation literacy should be taught in every school. Indeed, before the era of books, it was considered an absolutely core part of education,* albeit under an old-fashioned name: *rhetoric*. Today, in the connected era, we should resurrect that noble art and make it education's fourth *R*: reading, 'riting, 'rithmetic . . . and rhetoric.

The word's core meaning is simply "the art of speaking effectively." Fundamentally, that's the purpose of this book. To recast rhetoric for the modern era. To offer useful stepping-stones toward a new presentation literacy.

Our experience at TED over the last few years can help point the way. TED began as an annual conference, bringing together the fields of technology, entertainment, and design (hence the name). But in recent years it has expanded to cover any topic of public interest. TED speakers seek to make their ideas accessible to those outside their field by delivering short, carefully prepared talks. And to our delight, this form of public speaking has proved

---

* Along with logic, grammar, arithmetic, geometry, astronomy, and music.

a hit online, to the extent that, as of 2015, more than 1 billion TED Talks are viewed annually.

My colleagues and I have worked with hundreds of TED speakers, helping fine-tune their messages and how they deliver them. These amazing people have completely changed the way we see the world. Over the past decade, we have debated passionately among ourselves how exactly these speakers have achieved what they've achieved. From our lucky ringside seats, we have been intrigued and infuriated, informed and inspired. We have also had the chance to ask them directly for their advice on how to prepare and deliver an amazing talk. Thanks to their brilliance, we've learned dozens of insights into how they achieved something so extraordinary in just a few minutes.

That makes this book a collaborative effort. It's a collaboration with those speakers, and with my talented colleagues, especially Kelly Stoetzel, Bruno Giussani, and Tom Rielly, who curate and host the main TED events with me, and who have had a central role over the years in shaping the TED Talk approach and format and bringing remarkable voices to our platform.

We have also tapped into the collective wisdom of thousands of self-organized TEDx events.* The content emerging from them often surprises and delights us, and it has expanded our understanding of what is possible in a public talk.

TED's mission is to nurture the spread of powerful ideas. We don't care whether this is done through something called TED, TEDx, or in any other form of public speaking. When we hear of other conferences deciding they want to put on TED-style talks, we're thrilled. Ultimately, ideas aren't owned. They have a life of

---

* In TEDx, local organizers apply for a free license, allowing them to run a TED-like event in their locale. Some eight or nine such events are held every day somewhere in the world.

their own. We're delighted to see today's renaissance in the art of public speaking wherever it is happening and whoever is doing it.

So the purpose of this book is not just to describe how to give a TED Talk. It's much broader than that. Its purpose is to support any form of public speaking that seeks to explain, inspire, inform, or persuade; whether in business, education, or on the public stage. Yes, many of the examples in this book are from TED Talks, but that's not only because those are the examples we're most familiar with. TED Talks have generated a lot of excitement in recent years, and we think they have something to offer the wider world of public speaking. We think the principles that underlie them can act as a powerful basis for a broader presentation literacy.

So you won't find specific tips on giving a toast at a wedding, or a company sales pitch, or a university lecture. But you will find tools and insights that may be useful for those occasions and, indeed, for every form of public speaking. More than that, we hope to persuade you to think about public speaking in a different way, a way that you will find exciting and empowering.

The campfires of old have spawned a new kind of fire. A fire that spreads from mind to mind, screen to screen: the ignition of ideas whose time has come.

This matters. Every meaningful element of human progress has happened only because humans have shared ideas with each other and then collaborated to turn those ideas into reality. From the first time our ancestors teamed up to take down a mammoth to Neil Armstrong's first step onto the moon, people have turned spoken words into astonishing shared achievements.

We need that now more than ever. Ideas that could solve our toughest problems often remain invisible because the brilliant people in whose minds they reside lack the confidence or the know-how to share those ideas effectively. That is a tragedy. At a time when the right idea presented the right way can ripple across the world at the speed of light, spawning copies of itself in millions of minds, there's huge benefit to figuring out how best to set it on its way, both for you, the speaker-in-waiting, and for the rest of us who need to know what you have to say.

Are you ready?

Let's go light a fire.

Chris Anderson
February 2016

Foundation

1

PRESENTATION LITERACY
The Skill You Can Build

You're nervous, right?

Stepping out onto a public stage and having hundreds of pairs of eyes turned your way is terrifying. You dread having to stand up in a company meeting and present your project. What if you get nervous and stumble over your words? What if you completely forget what you were going to say? Maybe you'll be humiliated! Maybe your career will crater! Maybe the idea you believe in will stay buried forever!

These are thoughts that can keep you up at night.

But guess what? Almost everyone has experienced the fear of public speaking. Indeed, surveys that ask people to list their top fears often report public speaking as the most widely selected, ahead of snakes, heights — and even death.

How can this be? There is no tarantula hidden behind the microphone. You have zero risk of plunging off the stage to your death. The audience will not attack you with pitchforks. Then why the anxiety?

It's because there's a lot at stake — not just the experience in the moment, but in our longer-term *reputation*. How others think of us matters hugely. We are profoundly social animals. We crave each other's affection, respect, and support. Our future happiness depends on these realities to a shocking degree. And we sense that what happens on a public stage is going to materially affect these social currencies for better or worse.

But with the right mindset, you can use your fear as an incredible asset. It can be the driver that will persuade you to prepare for a talk properly.

That's what happened when Monica Lewinsky came to TED. For her, the stakes couldn't have been higher. Seventeen years earlier, she had been through the most humiliating public exposure imaginable, an experience so intense it almost broke her. Now she was attempting a return to a more visible public life, to reclaim her narrative.

But she was not an experienced public speaker, and she knew that it would be disastrous if she messed up. She told me:

> Nervous is too mild a word to describe how I felt. More like ... Gutted with trepidation. Bolts of fear. Electric anxiety. If we could have harnessed the power of my nerves that morning, I think the energy crisis would have been solved. Not only was I stepping out onto a stage in front of an esteemed and brilliant crowd, but it was also videotaped, with the high likelihood of being made public on a widely viewed platform. I was visited by the echoes of lingering trauma from years of having been publicly ridiculed. Plagued by a deep insecurity I didn't belong on the TED stage. That was the inner experience against which I battled.

And yet Monica found a way to turn that fear around. She used some surprising techniques, which I'll share in chapter 15. Suffice it to say, they worked. Her talk won a standing ovation at the event, rocketed to a million views within a few days, and earned rave reviews online. It even prompted a public apology to her from a longtime critic, feminist author Erica Jong.

The brilliant woman I am married to, Jacqueline Novogratz, was also haunted by fear of public speaking. In school, at college, and into her twenties, the prospect of a microphone and watching eyes was so scary it was debilitating. But she knew that to advance her work fighting poverty, she would have to persuade others, and so she just began forcing herself to do it. Today she gives scores of speeches every year, often earning standing ovations.

Indeed, everywhere you look, there are stories of people who were terrified of public speaking but found a way to become really good at it, from Eleanor Roosevelt to Warren Buffett to Princess Diana, who was known to all as "shy Di" and hated giving speeches, but found a way to speak informally in her own voice, and the world fell in love with her.

If you can get a talk right, the upside can be amazing. Take the talk that entrepreneur Elon Musk gave to SpaceX employees on August 2, 2008.

Musk was not known as a great public speaker. But that day, his words marked an important turning point for his company. SpaceX had already suffered two failed launches. This was the day of the third launch, and everyone knew failure could force the company's closure. The *Falcon* rocket soared off the launch pad, but right after the first stage fell away, disaster struck. The spacecraft exploded. The video feed went dead. Some 350 employees had gathered and, as described by Dolly Singh, the company's head of talent acquisition, the mood was thick with despair. Musk emerged to speak to them. He told them they'd always known it would be hard, but that despite what had happened, they had already accomplished something that day that few nations, let alone companies, had achieved. They had successfully completed the first stage of a launch and taken a spacecraft to outer space. They simply had to pick themselves up and get back to work. Here's how Singh described the talk's climax:

> Then Elon said, with as much fortitude and ferocity as he could muster after having been awake for like 20+ hours by this point, "For my part, I will never give up and I mean never." I think most of us would have followed him into the gates of hell car-

rying suntan oil after that. It was the most impressive display of leadership that I have ever witnessed. Within moments the energy of the building went from despair and defeat to a massive buzz of determination as people began to focus on moving forward instead of looking back.

That's the power of a single talk. You might not be leading an organization, but a talk can still open new doors or transform a career.

TED speakers have told us delightful stories of the impact of their talks. Yes, there are sometimes book and movie offers, higher speaking fees, and unexpected offers of financial support. But the most appealing stories are of ideas advanced, and lives changed. Amy Cuddy gave a hugely popular talk about how changing your body language can raise your confidence level. She has had more than 15,000 messages from people around the world, telling her how that wisdom has helped them.

And young Malawian inventor William Kamkwamba's inspiring talk about building a windmill in his village as a fourteen-year-old sparked a series of events that led to him being accepted into an engineering program at Dartmouth College.

THE DAY TED MIGHT HAVE DIED

Here's a story from my own life: When I first took over leadership of TED in late 2001, I was reeling from the near collapse of the company I had spent fifteen years building, and I was terrified of another huge public failure. I had been struggling to persuade the TED community to back my vision for TED, and I feared that it might just fizzle out. Back then, TED was an annual conference in California, owned and hosted by a charismatic architect named Richard Saul Wurman, whose larger-than-life presence infused every aspect of the conference. About eight hundred people attended every year, and most of them seemed resigned to the fact that TED probably couldn't survive once Wurman departed. The TED conference of February 2002 was the last one to be held under his leadership, and I had one chance and one chance only to persuade TED attendees that the conference would continue just fine. I had never run a conference before, however, and despite my best efforts over several months at marketing the following year's event, only seventy people had signed up for it.

Early on the last morning of that conference, I had 15 minutes to make my case. And here's what you need to know about me: I am not naturally a great speaker. I say *um* and *you know* far too often. I will stop halfway through a sentence, trying to find the right word to continue. I can sound overly earnest, soft-spoken, conceptual. My quirky British sense of humor is not always shared by others.

I was so nervous about this moment, and so worried that I would look awkward on the stage, that I couldn't even bring myself to stand. Instead I rolled forward a chair from the back of the stage, sat on it, and began.

I look back at that talk now and cringe — a lot. If I were critiquing it today, there are a hundred things I would change, starting with the wrinkly white T-shirt I was wearing. And yet . . . I had prepared carefully what I wanted to say, and I knew there were at least some in the audience desperate for TED to survive. If I could just give those supporters a reason to get excited, perhaps they would turn things around. Because of the recent dot-com bust, many in the audience had suffered business losses as bad as my own. Maybe I could connect with them that way?

I spoke from the heart, with as much openness and conviction as I could summon. I told people I had just gone through a massive business failure. That I'd come to think of myself as a complete loser. That the only way I'd survived mentally was by immersing myself in the world of ideas. That TED had come to mean the world to me—that it was a unique place where ideas from every discipline could be shared. That I would do all in my power to preserve its best values. That, in any case, the conference had brought such intense inspiration and learning to us that we couldn't possibly let it die . . . could we?

Oh, and I broke the tension with an apocryphal anecdote about France's Madame de Gaulle and how she shocked guests at a diplomatic dinner by expressing her desire for *"a penis."* In England, I said, we also had that desire, although there we pronounced it *happiness,* and TED had brought genuine happiness my way.

To my utter amazement, at the end of the talk, Jeff Bezos, the head of Amazon, who was seated in the center of the audience, rose to his feet and began clapping. And the whole room stood with him. It was as if the TED community had collectively decided, in just a few seconds, that it would support this new chapter of TED after all. And in the 60-minute break that followed, some 200 people committed to buying passes for the following year's conference, guaranteeing its success.

If that 15-minute talk had fizzled, TED would have died, four years before ever putting a talk on the Internet. You would not be reading this book.

In the next chapter, I'll share why I think that talk ended up being effective, despite its evident awkwardness. It's an insight that can be applied to any talk.

No matter how little confidence you might have today in your ability to speak in public, there are things you can do to turn that around. Facility with public speaking is not a gift granted at birth to a lucky few. It's a broad-ranging set of skills. There are hundreds of ways to give a talk, and everyone can find an approach that's right for them and learn the skills necessary to do it well.

THE BOY WITH THE LION-HEART

A couple of years ago, TED's content director, Kelly Stoetzel, and I went on a global tour in search of speaking talent. In Nairobi, Kenya, we met Richard Turere, a twelve-year-old Maasai boy who had come up with a surprising invention. His family raised cattle, and one of the biggest challenges was protecting them at night from lion attacks. Richard had noticed that a stationary campfire didn't deter the lions, but walking around waving a torch did seem to work. The lions were apparently afraid of moving lights! Richard had somehow taught himself electronics by messing around with parts taken from his parents' radio. He used that knowledge to devise a system of lights that would turn on and off in sequence, creating a sense of movement. It was built from scrapyard parts — solar panels, a car battery, and a motorcycle indicator box. He installed the lights and — presto! — the lion attacks stopped. News of his invention spread and other villages wanted in. Instead of seeking to kill the lions as they had done before, they installed Richard's "lion lights." Both villagers and pro-lion environmentalists were happy.

It was an impressive achievement but, at first glance, Richard certainly seemed an unlikely TED speaker. He stood hunched over in a corner of the room, painfully shy. His English was halting, and he struggled to describe his invention coherently. It was hard to imagine him on a stage in California in front of 1,400 people, slotted alongside Sergey Brin and Bill Gates.

But Richard's story was so compelling that we went ahead anyway and invited him to come give a TED Talk. In the months before the conference, we worked with him to frame his story — to find the right place to begin, and to develop a natural narrative sequence. Because of his invention, Richard had won a scholarship to one of Kenya's best schools, where he had the chance to practice his TED Talk several times in front of a live audience. This helped build his confidence to the point where his personality could shine through.

He got on an airplane for the first time in his life and flew to Long Beach, California. As he walked onto the TED stage, you could tell he was nervous, but that only made him more engaging. As Richard spoke, people were hanging on his every word, and every time he smiled, the audience melted. When he finished, people just stood and cheered.

Richard's tale can encourage us all to believe we might be able to give a decent talk. Your goal is not to be Winston Churchill or Nelson Mandela. It's to be you. If you're a scientist, be a scientist; don't try to be an activist. If you're an artist, be an artist; don't try to be an academic. If you're just an ordinary person, don't try to fake some big intellectual style; just be you. You don't have to raise a crowd to its feet with a thunderous oration. Conversational sharing can work just as well. In fact, for most audiences, it's a lot better. If you know how to talk to a group of friends over dinner, then you know enough to speak publicly.

And technology is opening up new options. We live in an age where you don't have to be able to speak to thousands of people at a time to have an outsized impact. It could just be you talking intimately to a video camera, and letting the Internet do the rest.

Presentation literacy isn't an optional extra for the few. It's a core skill for the twenty-first century. It's the most impactful way to share who you are and what you care about. If you can learn to do it, your self-confidence will flourish, and you may be amazed at the beneficial impact it can have on your success in life, however you might choose to define that.

If you commit to being the authentic you, I am certain that you will be capable of tapping into the ancient art that is wired inside us. You simply have to pluck up the courage to try.

2

IDEA BUILDING

The Gift in Every Great Talk

In March 2015, a scientist named Sophie Scott stepped onto the TED stage, and within 2 minutes the entire audience was howling with uncontrollable laughter. Sophie is one of the world's leading researchers on laughter, and she was playing an audio clip of humans laughing and showing just how *weird* a phenomenon it is — "more like an animal call than speech," as she put it.

Her talk was 17 minutes of pure delight. By the end of it, everyone was basking in the warm glow of a deeply pleasurable experience. But there was something else. None of us would ever think of laughter in quite the same way again. Sophie's core *idea* about laughter — that its evolutionary purpose is to convert social stress into pleasurable alignment — had somehow entered our heads. And now, whenever I see a group of people laughing, I see the phenomenon through new eyes. Yes, I feel the joy, I feel the urge to join in. But I also see social bonding, and a strange and ancient biological phenomenon at work that makes the whole thing seem even more wondrous.

Sophie gave me a gift. Not just the pleasure of listening to her. She gave me an idea that can forever be part of me.*

---

* Of course, Sophie Scott's idea may get refined or contradicted by future research. In that sense, ideas are always provisional. But once an idea is formed in our minds, no one can take it from us without our consent.

I'd like to suggest that Sophie's gift is a beautiful metaphor that can apply to any talk. *Your number-one mission as a speaker is to take something that matters deeply to you and to rebuild it inside the minds of your listeners.* We'll call that something an *idea*. A mental construct that they can hold on to, walk away with, value, and in some sense be changed by.

That is the core reason that the scariest talk I ever had to give turned out to be effective. As I explained earlier, I had 15 minutes to try to convince the TED audience to support its new chapter under my leadership. There were many things wrong with that talk, but it succeeded in one key aspect: It planted an idea inside the minds of those listening. It was the idea that what was truly special about TED was not just the founder I was taking over from. TED's uniqueness lay in being a place where people from every discipline could come together and understand each other. This cross-fertilization really mattered for the world, and therefore the conference would be given nonprofit status and held in trust for the public good. Its future was for all of us.

This idea changed the way the audience thought about the TED transition. It no longer mattered so much that the founder was leaving. What mattered now was that a special way of sharing knowledge should be preserved.

START WITH THE IDEA

The central thesis of this book is that anyone who has an idea worth sharing is capable of giving a powerful talk. The only thing that truly matters in public speaking is not confidence, stage presence, or smooth talking. It's having something worth saying.

I am using the word *idea* quite broadly here. It doesn't have to be a scientific breakthrough, a genius invention, or a complex legal theory. It can be a simple how-to. Or a human insight illustrated with the power of a story. Or a beautiful image that has meaning. Or an event you wish might happen in the future. Or perhaps just a reminder of what matters most in life.

An idea is anything that can change how people see the world. If you can conjure up a compelling idea in people's minds, you have done something wondrous. You have given them a gift of incalculable value. In a very real sense, a little piece of you has become part of them.

Do *you* have ideas that deserve a wider audience? It's amazing how bad we are at judging an answer to that question. A lot of speakers (often male) appear to love the sound of their own voice and are happy to talk for hours without sharing anything much of value. But there are also many people (often female) who massively underestimate the value of their work, and their learning, and their insights.

If you've picked up this book just because you love the idea of strutting the stage and being a TED Talk star, inspiring audiences with your charisma, please, put it down right now. Instead, go and work on something that is worth sharing. Style without substance is awful.

But, more likely, you have far more in you worth sharing than you're even aware of. You don't have to have invented lion lights. You've led a life that is yours and yours only. There are experiences you've had that are unique to you. There are insights to be drawn from some of those experiences that are absolutely worth sharing. You just have to figure out which ones.

Are you stressed about this? Maybe you have a class assignment; or you need to present the results of your research at a small meeting; or you have a chance to speak to a local Rotary about your organization and try to gain their support. You may feel that you've done nothing that would be worth giving a talk about. You've invented nothing. You're not particularly creative. You don't see yourself as super-intelligent. You don't have any particularly brilliant ideas about the future. You're not even sure there's anything you're super-passionate about.

Well, I grant you, that's a tough starting point. To be worth an audience's time, most talks require grounding in something that has some depth. It's theoretically possible that the best thing you can do for now is to continue your journey, search for something that really does grab you and make you want to go deep, and pick up this book again in a few years' time.

But before you come to that conclusion, it's worth double-checking that your self-assessment is accurate. Maybe you're just lacking self-confidence. There's a paradox here: You have always been you, and you only see yourself from the inside. The bits that others find remarkable in you may be completely invisible to you. To find those bits you may need to have honest conversations with those who know you best. They will know some parts of you better than you know them yourself.

In any case, there's one thing you have that no one else in the world has: Your own first-person experience of life. Yesterday you saw a sequence of things and experienced a sequence of emotions that is, quite literally, unique. You are the only human among 7 billion who had that exact experience. So . . . can you make anything of that? Many of the best talks are simply based on a personal story and a simple lesson to be drawn from it. Did you observe anything that surprised you? Maybe you watched a couple of children playing in the park, or had a conversation with a homeless person. Is there something in what you saw that might be interesting to other people? If not, could you imagine spending the next few weeks walking around with your eyes open, being aware of the possibility that some part of your unique journey could be of interest and benefit to others?

People love stories, and everyone can learn to tell a good story. Even if the lesson you might draw from the story is familiar, that's OK — we're humans! We need reminding! There's a reason religions have weekly sermons that tell us the same things over and over, packaged different ways. An important idea, wrapped up in a fresh story, can make a great talk, if it's told the right way.

Think back over your work of the last three or four years; what really stands out? What was the last thing you were really excited by? Or angered by? What are the two or three things you've done that you're most proud of? When was the last time you were in conversation with someone who said, "That's really interesting"? If you could wave a magic wand, what is the one idea you'd most love to spread to other people's minds?

PROCRASTINATE NO MORE

You can use the opportunity of public speaking as *motivation* to dive more deeply into some topic. We all suffer, to a greater or lesser degree, from some form of procrastination or laziness. There's a lot we'd like to get into in principle, but, you know, that Internet thing just has so many damn distractions. The chance to speak in public may be just the kick you need to commit to a serious research project. Anyone with a computer or a smartphone has access to pretty much all the world's information. It's just a matter of digging in and seeing what you can uncover.

In fact, the same questions you ask as you do your research can help provide the blueprint for your talk. What are the issues that matter most? How are they related? How can they be easily explained? What are the riddles that people don't yet have good answers for? What are the key controversies? You can use your own journey of discovery to suggest your talk's key moments of revelation.

So, if you think you *might* have something but aren't sure you really know enough yet, why not use your public-speaking opportunity as an incentive to truly find out? Every time you feel your attention flagging, just remember the prospect of standing on stage with hundreds of eyes peering at you. That will get you through the next hour of effort!

In 2015, we tried an experiment at TED headquarters. We granted everyone on the team an extra day off every second week to devote to studying something. We called it Learning Wednesdays. The idea was that, because the organization is committed to lifelong learning, we should practice what we preach and encourage everyone on the team to spend time learning about something they're passionate about. But how did we prevent that just becoming a lazy day of sitting in front of the TV? There was a sting in the tail: Everyone had to commit, at some point during the year, to giving a TED Talk to the rest of the organization about what they've learned. That meant we all got to benefit from one another's knowledge but, crucially, it also provided the key incentive for people to get on with it and actually learn.

You don't need Learning Wednesdays to have this motivation. Any chance at speaking to a group you respect can provide the incentive you need to get off your butt and work on something unique to you! In other words, you don't need to have the perfect knowledge in your head today. Use this opportunity as the reason to discover it.

And if, after all that, you're still floundering, maybe you're right. Maybe you should turn down the offer to speak. You might be doing yourself — and them — a favor. More likely, though, you'll land on something that you, and only you, can share. Something you'd actually be excited to see out there in the world a little more visibly.

For most of the rest of this book, I'm going to assume that you have something you want to talk about, whether it's a lifelong passion, a topic you're eager to dive into more deeply, or a project for work that you have to present. In the chapters to come

I'll be focusing on the *how*, not the *what*. But in the final chapter we'll return to the what, because I'm pretty sure that *everyone* has something important they could and should share with the rest of us.

THE ASTONISHING EFFICACY OF LANGUAGE

OK. You have something meaningful to say, and your goal is to re-create your core idea inside your audience's minds. How do you do that?

We shouldn't underestimate how challenging that is. If we could somehow map what that idea about laughter looked like in Sophie Scott's brain, it would probably involve millions of neurons interconnected in an incredibly rich and complex pattern. The pattern would have to include, somehow, images of people guffawing, the sounds that they make, the concepts of evolutionary purpose and of what it means to ease stress, and much more. How on earth is it possible to re-create that whole structure in a group of strangers' minds in just a few minutes?

Humans have developed a technology that makes this possible. It's called *language*. It makes your brain do incredible things.

I want you to imagine an elephant, with its trunk painted bright red, waving it to and fro in sync with the shuffling steps of a giant orange parrot dancing on the elephant's head and shrieking over and over again, "Let's do the fandango!"

Wow! You have just formed in your mind an image of something that has never existed in history, except in my mind and in the minds of others who read that last sentence. A single sentence can do that. But it depends on you, the listener, having a set of preexisting concepts. You must already know what an elephant and a parrot are, what the color concepts of red and orange are, and what *painted, dancing,* and *in sync* mean. That sentence has prompted you to link those concepts into a brand-new pattern.

If I had instead started out by saying *"I want you to imagine a member of the species* Loxodonta cyclotis, *with proboscis pigmented Pantone 032U, conducting oscillatory motions . . ."* you probably would not have formed that image, even though this is the same request in more precise language.

So, language works its magic only to the extent that it is shared by speaker and listener. And there's the key clue to how to achieve the miracle of re-creating your idea in someone else's brain. *You can only use the tools that your audience has access to.* If you start only with *your* language, *your* concepts, *your* assumptions, *your* values, you will fail. So instead, start with theirs. It's only from that common ground that they can begin to build *your* idea inside *their* minds.

At Princeton University, Dr. Uri Hasson has been doing groundbreaking research to try to discover how this process works. It's possible to capture in real time the complex brain activity associated with building a concept or remembering a story. It requires a technology called *functional magnetic resonance imaging* (fMRI).

In one experiment in 2015, Dr. Hasson put a group of volunteers into fMRI machines and played them a 50-minute film that told a story. As they experienced the story, their brains' response patterns were recorded. Some of those patterns could be matched across almost every volunteer, giving concrete physical evidence of the shared experience they were having. Then he asked the volunteers to record their own recollections of the film. Many of these recordings were quite detailed and lasted as long as 20 minutes. Now — and this is the astounding part — he played those recordings to another set of volunteers who had never seen the film, and recorded *their* fMRI data. The patterns shown in the brains of the second set of volunteers, those who listened to the audio rec-ollections only, matched those patterns shown in the minds of the first set of volunteers as they watched the movie! In other words, the power of language alone conjured up the same mental experi-ences that others had while watching a movie.

This is amazing evidence of language's efficacy. It is a power that every public speaker can tap into.

YES, WORDS MATTER

Some public-speaking coaches seek to downplay the importance of language. They may cite research published in 1967 by Profes-sor Albert Mehrabian and claim that only 7 percent of the effec-tiveness of communication is down to language, while 38 percent depends on tone of voice and 55 percent comes from body lan-guage. This has led coaches to focus excessively on developing a speaking style of confidence, charisma, etc., and not worry so much about the words.

Unfortunately, this is a complete misinterpretation of what Mehrabian found. His experiments were devoted primarily to discovering how *emotion* was communicated. So for example, he would test what would happen if someone said "That's nice," but said so in an angry tone of voice, or with threatening body language. Sure enough, in those circumstances, the words don't count for much. But it is absurd to apply this to speaking over-all (and Mehrabian is so sick of being misapplied that his website contains a bolded paragraph begging people not to do this).

Yes, communicating emotion is important, and for that aspect of a talk, one's tone of voice and body language do indeed mat-ter a great deal. We discuss this in detail in later chapters. But the whole substance of a talk depends crucially on words. It's the words that tell a story, build an idea, explain the complex, make a reasoned case, or provide a compelling call to action. So, if you hear someone tell you that body language matters more than verbal language in public speaking, please know that they are misinterpreting the science. (Or for fun, you could just ask them to repeat their point purely with gestures!)

We'll spend much of the first half of this book digging into ways in which language can achieve its magic. The fact that we can transfer ideas in this way is why human-to-human speaking matters. It is how our worldviews are built and shaped. Our ideas make us who we are. And speakers who have figured out how to spread their ideas into others' minds are able to create ripple effects of untold consequence.

THE JOURNEY

There's one other beautiful metaphor for a great talk. It is a *journey* that speaker and audience take together. Speaker Tierney Thys puts it this way:

> Like all good movies or books, a great talk is transporting. We love to go on adventures, travel someplace new with an informed, if not quirky, guide who can introduce us to things we never knew existed, incite us to crawl out windows into strange worlds, outfit us with new lenses to see the ordinary in an extraordinary way . . . enrapture us and engage multiple parts of our brains simultaneously. So I often try to fashion my talks around embarking on a journey.

What's powerful about this metaphor is that it makes clear why the speaker, like any tour guide, must begin where the audience is. And why they must ensure no impossible leaps or inexplicable shifts in direction.

Whether the journey is one of exploration, explanation, or persuasion, the net result is to have brought the audience to a beautiful new place. And that too is a gift.

Whichever metaphor you use, focusing on what you will *give* to your audience is the perfect foundation for preparing your talk.

3

COMMON TRAPS

Four Talk Styles to Avoid

There are countless ways to build a great talk. But first some essential safety tips. There are ugly talk styles out there, dangerous to both a speaker's reputation and an audience's well-being. Here are four to steer clear of at all costs.

THE SALES PITCH

Sometimes speakers get it exactly backwards. They plan to take, not give.

Several years ago a famed author and business consultant came to TED. I was excited to hear his presentation on how to think outside the box. What happened instead horrified me. He began talking about a series of businesses that had apparently made a significant leap forward as a result of an action they took. And what was that action? They had all booked his consultancy services.

After 5 minutes of this, the audience was getting antsy and I'd had enough. I stood up and began to interrupt. Every eye turned my way. I was sweating. My microphone was on. Everyone could hear everything.

Me: I have a request here. Perhaps you could tell us about the actual type of thinking you recommend? We want to

know how it actually works, so that we've got a takeaway. As is, it's a bit too much of an ad.
[*Nervous applause. Awkward pause.*]

Speaker: It takes three days to go into it. In 15 minutes, there is no way I can tell you all about how to do it. My purpose is to tell you that these things can work and therefore motivate you to look further into them.

Me: We believe you that they work. You're a rock star in this field! Give us an instance, or just tease us with the first 15 minutes of it. Please!

At this point, the audience starts cheering and the speaker's left with no choice. To everyone's relief, he finally begins to share some wisdom we can use.

Here's the irony. This greedy approach to speaking doesn't even serve the speaker's interest. I'd be amazed if he got a single booking from anyone in that audience. And even if he did, it had to be offset by a loss of respect from others in the room. Needless to say, we never posted the talk online.

Reputation is everything. You want to build a reputation as a generous person, bringing something wonderful to your audiences, not as a tedious self-promoter. It's boring and frustrating to be pitched to, especially when you're expecting something else.

Usually, of course, pitches happen much more subtly. The slide showing a book cover; the brief mention about the speaker's organization's funding shortfall. In the context of an otherwise great talk, you may even get away with these little nudges. (And, of course, if you've been specifically asked to talk about the book or the organization, that's another matter.) But you're taking a big risk. That's why at TED we actively discourage speakers from doing these things.

The key principle is to remember that the speaker's job is to *give* to the audience, not take from them. (Even in a business context where you're genuinely making a sales pitch, your goal should be to give. The most effective salespeople put themselves into their listeners' shoes and imagine how to best serve their needs.) At a conference, people don't come to a talk to be sold to. As soon as they understand that might be your agenda, they will flee to the safety of their email inbox. It's as if you've agreed to have a coffee with a friend and discover to your horror that all she actually wanted to do was explain her must-invest time-share scheme to you. You're out of there at the first opportunity.

It's possible to disagree where the line is between sharing an idea and pitching, but the principle is crucial: Give, don't take.

And here's the thing. Generosity evokes a response. When human-rights lawyer Bryan Stevenson spoke at TED, his organization was in urgent need of $1 million to continue fighting a key case in the US Supreme Court. But Bryan didn't mention this once in his talk. Instead he transformed the way we all thought about injustice in America, offering stories, insights, humor, and revelation. At the end the audience rose as one and applauded for several minutes. And guess what? He left the conference with contributions from attendees exceeding $1.3 million.

THE RAMBLE

In the first TED I organized, one of the speakers began, "As I was driving down here wondering what to say to you . . ." There followed an unfocused list of observations about possible futures. Nothing obnoxious. Nothing that was particularly hard to understand. But also no arguments of power. No revelations. No aha moments. No takeaways. The audience clapped politely. But no one really learned anything.

I was fuming. It's one thing to underprepare. But to boast that you've underprepared? That's insulting. It tells the audience that their time doesn't matter. That the event doesn't matter.

So many talks are like this. Meandering, no clear direction. A speaker might kid himself that even an unfocused exploration of his brilliant thinking is bound to be fascinating to others. But if 800 people are planning to devote 15 minutes of their day to your words, you really can't just wing it.

As my colleague Bruno Giussani puts it, "When people sit in a room to listen to a speaker, they are offering her something extremely precious, something that isn't recoverable once given: a few minutes of their time and of their attention. Her task is to use that time as well as possible."

So if you're going to gift people with a wondrous idea, you first have to spend some preparation time. Rambling is not an option.

As it turned out, this particular rambling speaker did give TED a gift of sorts. From that talk on, we redoubled our efforts on speaker preparation.

THE ORG BORE

An organization is fascinating to those who work for it — and deeply boring to almost everyone else. Sorry, but it's true. Any talk framed around the exceptional history of your company or NGO or lab and the complex-but-oh-so-impressive way it is structured, and the fabulously photogenic quality of the astonishingly talented team working with you, and how much success your products are having, is going to leave your audience snoozing at the starting line. It may be interesting to you and your team. But, alas, we don't work there.

Everything changes, though, when you focus on the nature of

the work that you're doing, and the power of the ideas that infuse it, not on the org itself or its products.

This can be harder than it sounds. Ofttimes the heads of organizations are by default their spokespersons, always in selling mode, believing it's their obligation to honor the hard-working team that surrounds them. And because the work they want to talk about has taken place inside the organization, the most obvious way to describe it may be to anchor it to organizational acts. "Back in 2005, we set up a new department in Dallas in this office building *[slide of glass tower here],* and its goal was to investigate how we could slash our energy costs, so I allocated Vice President Hank Boreham to the task . . ." Yawn.

Compare that statement to this one: "Back in 2005 we discovered something surprising. It turns out that it's possible for an average office to slash its energy costs by 60 percent without any noticeable loss of productivity. Let me share with you how . . ."

One mode retains interest. One kills it. One mode is a gift. The other is lazily self-serving.

THE INSPIRATION PERFORMANCE

I hesitate to include this example, but I think I must.

Let's agree on this first: Absolutely one of the most powerful things you can experience when watching a talk is *inspiration.* The speaker's work and words move you and fill you with an expanded sense of possibility and excitement. You want to go out and be a better person. TED's growth and success have been fueled by the deeply inspirational nature of many of the talks. Indeed, it's the reason I was drawn to TED in the first place. I believe in inspiration's power.

But it's a power that must be handled with great care.

When a great speaker finishes her talk and the whole crowd

rises to its feet and applauds, it's a thrilling moment for everyone in the room. The audience is excited by what they've heard, and for the speaker, it's indescribably satisfying to receive such powerful recognition. (One of the more awkward moments we've ever had at TED was when a speaker left the stage to lukewarm applause and whispered to her friend backstage, "Nobody stood up!" An understandable comment. It was just unfortunate that her microphone was still on, and everyone could hear the pain in her voice.)

Whether they admit it or not, many public speakers dream of being cheered as they leave the stage, followed by screens full of tweets attesting to their inspirational prowess. And therein lies the trap. The intense appeal of the standing ovation can lead aspiring speakers to do bad things. They may look at talks given by inspirational speakers and seek to copy them . . . but in form only. The result can be awful: the ruthless pursuit of every trick in the book to intellectually and emotionally manipulate the audience.

There was an upsetting instance of this at TED a few years ago.* An American man in his forties had become a huge TED fan, and he sent us a compelling audition video, urging us to let him give his own talk. His talk premise exactly matched the theme we were focused on that year, and he came well recommended, so we decided to give him a shot.

The first moments of his talk were promising. He had a big personality. He beamed at the audience. He had some amusing opening remarks, a clever video, and a surprising visual prop. It was as if he'd studied every TED Talk in detail and was bringing the best of each to his own talk. Sitting and watching, I was hopeful we might have a giant hit on our hands.

But then . . . I started to feel a little queasy. There was some-

---

* To be kind, I've changed a couple of details.

thing not quite right. He was loving being on stage. Loving it just a little too much. He'd keep pausing, hoping for audience applause or laughter, and when he got it, he'd stop and say "thank you," subtly milking it for more. He started inserting ad-libbed comments intended to amuse. It was clear they amused him, but others, not so much. And the worst of it was the promised substance of the talk never really arrived. He claimed to have worked on demonstrating the truth of an important idea. But the case he brought was all whimsy and anecdote. There was one moment where he had even Photoshopped an image so that it appeared to support his case. And because of his getting carried away and soaking up the limelight, he was running way overtime.

Toward the end, he began telling people that yes, they had it in their power to adopt his wisdom, and he spoke of dreams and inspiration, ending with his arms outstretched to the audience. Because it was clear the talk meant so much to him, a portion of the audience did indeed stand to clap him. Me? I felt sick to my stomach. This was the cliché of TED that we'd tried so hard to eliminate. All style, very little substance.

The trouble with talks like this is not just that they flatter to deceive. It's that they give the entire genre a bad name. They make the audience less likely to open up when a genuinely inspiring speaker comes along. And yet, more and more speakers, attracted to the drug of audience adoration, are trying to walk this path.

Please don't be one of them.

Here's the thing about inspiration: It has to be earned. Someone is inspiring not because they look at you with big eyes and ask you to find it in your heart to believe in their dream. It's because they actually have a dream that's worth getting excited about. And those dreams don't come lightly. They come from blood, sweat, and tears.

Inspiration is like love. You don't get it by pursuing it directly. In fact, there's a name for people who pursue love too directly: *stalker*. In less extreme cases, the words we use are almost as bad: *cloying, inappropriate, desperate*. And sadly, this behavior prompts the opposite of what it desires. It prompts a pulling back.

It's the same with inspiration. If you try to take the shortcut and win people over purely with your charisma, you may succeed for a moment or two, but soon you'll be found out, and the audience will flee. In the example above, despite the partial standing ovation, that speaker received terrible audience feedback in our postconference survey, and we never posted the talk. People had felt manipulated. And they were.

If you have dreams of being a rock-star public speaker, pumping up an audience as you stride the stage and proclaim your brilliance, I beg you to reconsider. Don't dream of that. Dream of something much bigger than you are. Go and work on that dream as long as it takes to achieve something worthwhile. And then humbly come and share what you've learned.

Inspiration can't be performed. It's an audience response to authenticity, courage, selfless work, and genuine wisdom. Bring those qualities to your talk, and you may be amazed at what happens.

It's easy to talk about why talks fail. But how can they be built to succeed? It all starts with a moment of clarity.

4
THE THROUGHLINE
What's Your Point?

"It happens way too often: you're sitting there in the audience, listening to someone talk, and you know that there is a better and great talk in that person, it's just not the talk he's giving." That's TED's Bruno Giussani again, a man who cannot stand seeing potentially great speakers blow their opportunity.

The point of a talk is . . . to say something meaningful. But it's amazing how many talks never quite do that. There are lots of spoken sentences, to be sure. But somehow they leave the audience with nothing they can hold on to. Beautiful slides and a charismatic stage presence are all very well, but if there's no real takeaway, all the speaker has done — at best — is to entertain.

The number-one reason for this tragedy is that the speaker never had a proper plan for the talk as a whole. The talk may have been planned bullet point by bullet point, or even sentence by sentence, but no time was actually spent on its overall arc.

There's a helpful word used to analyze plays, movies, and novels; it applies to talks too. It is *throughline,* the connecting theme that ties together each narrative element. Every talk should have one.

Since your goal is to construct something wondrous inside your listeners' minds, you can think of the throughline as a strong cord or rope, onto which you will attach all the elements that are part of the idea you're building.

This doesn't mean every talk can only cover one topic, tell a single story, or just proceed in one direction without diversions. Not at all. It just means that all the pieces need to connect.

Here's the start of a talk thrown together without a throughline. *"I want to share with you some experiences I had during my recent trip to Cape Town, and then make a few observations about life on the road . . ."*

Compare that with: *"On my recent trip to Cape Town, I learned something new about strangers — when you can trust them, and when you definitely can't. Let me share with you two very different experiences I had . . ."*

The first setup might work for your family. But the second, with its throughline visible from the get-go, is far more enticing to a general audience.

A good exercise is to try to encapsulate your throughline in no more than fifteen words. And those fifteen words need to provide robust content. It's not enough to think of your goal as, "I want to inspire the audience" or "I want to win support for my work." It has to be more focused than that. What is the precise idea you want to build inside your listeners? What is their takeaway?

It's also important not to have a throughline that's too predictable or banal, such as "the importance of hard work" or "the four main projects I've been working on." Zzzzz . . . You can do better! Here are the throughlines of some popular TED Talks. Notice that there's an *unexpectedness* incorporated into each of them.

- More choice actually makes us less happy.
- Vulnerability is something to be treasured, not hidden from.
- Education's potential is transformed if you focus on the amazing (and hilarious) creativity of kids.
- With body language, you can fake it till you become it.
- A history of the universe in 18 minutes shows a path from chaos to order.

- Terrible city flags can reveal surprising design secrets.
- A ski trek to the South Pole threatened my life and over-turned my sense of purpose.
- Let's bring on a quiet revolution — a world redesigned for introverts.
- The combination of three simple technologies creates a mind-blowing sixth sense.
- Online videos can humanize the classroom and revolution-ize education.

Barry Schwartz, whose talk is the first one in the list above, on the paradox of choice, is a big believer in the importance of a throughline:

> Many speakers have fallen in love with their ideas and find it hard to imagine what is complicated about them to people who are not already immersed. The key is to present just one idea — as thoroughly and completely as you can in the limited time period. What is it that you want your audience to have an unambiguous understanding of after you're done?

The last throughline in the list above is from education re-former Salman Khan. He told me:

> There were a lot of really interesting things that Khan Acad-emy had done, but that felt too self-serving. I wanted to share ideas that are bigger, ideas like mastery-based learning and hu-manizing class time by removing lectures. My advice to speak-ers would be to look for a single big idea that is larger than you or your organization, but at the same time to leverage your ex-perience to show that it isn't just empty speculation.

Your throughline doesn't have to be as ambitious as those above. But it still should have some kind of intriguing angle. Instead of giving a talk about the importance of hard work, how about speaking on why hard work sometimes *fails* to achieve true success, and what you can do about that. Instead of planning to speak about the four main projects you've recently been working on, how about structuring it around just three of the projects that happen to have a surprising connection?

In fact, Robin Murphy had exactly that as her throughline when she came to speak at TEDWomen. Here's the opening of her talk.

> Robots are quickly becoming first responders at disaster sites, working alongside humans to aid recovery. The involvement of these sophisticated machines has the potential to transform disaster relief, saving lives and money. I'd like to share with you today three new robots I've worked on that demonstrate this.

Not every talk has to state its throughline explicitly up front like this. As we'll see, there are many other ways to intrigue people and invite them to join you on your journey. But when the audience knows where you're headed, it's much easier for them to follow.

Let's think once again of a talk as a journey, a journey that the speaker and the audience take together, with the speaker as the guide. But if you, the speaker, want the audience to come with you, you probably need to give them a hint of where you're going. And then you need to be sure that each step of the journey helps get you there. In this journey metaphor, *the throughline traces the path that the journey takes*. It ensures that there are no impossible leaps, and that by the end of the talk, the speaker and audience have arrived together at a satisfying destination.

Many people approach a talk thinking they will just outline their work or describe their organization or explore an issue. That's not a great plan. The talk is likely to end up unfocused and without much impact.

Bear in mind that a throughline is not the same thing as a topic. Your invitation might seem super-clear. "Dear Mary. We want you to come talk about that new desalination technology you developed." "Dear John. Could you come tell us the story of your kayaking adventure in Kazakhstan?" But even when the *topic* is clear, the *throughline* is worth thinking about. A talk about kayaking could have a throughline based on endurance or group dynamics or the dangers of turbulent river eddies. The desalination talk might have a throughline based on disruptive innovation, or the global water crisis, or the awesomeness of engineering elegance.

So how do you figure out your throughline?

The first step is to find out as much as you can about the audience. Who are they? How knowledgeable are they? What are their expectations? What do they care about? What have past speakers there spoken about? You can only gift an idea to minds that are ready to receive that type of idea. If you're going to speak to an audience of taxi drivers in London about the amazingness of a digitally powered sharing economy, it would be helpful to know in advance that their livelihood is being destroyed by Uber.

But the biggest obstacle in identifying a throughline is expressed in every speaker's primal scream: *I have far too much to say and not enough time to say it!*

We hear this one a lot. TED Talks have a maximum time limit of 18 minutes. (Why 18? It's short enough to hold people's attention, including on the Internet, and precise enough to be taken seriously. But it's also long enough to say something that matters.) Yet most speakers are used to talking for 30 to 40 minutes or longer. They find it really hard to imagine giving a proper talk in such a short period of time.

It's certainly not the case that a shorter talk means shorter preparation time. President Woodrow Wilson was once asked about how long it took him to prepare for a speech. He replied:

That depends on the length of the speech. If it is a 10-minute speech it takes me all of two weeks to prepare it; if it is a half-hour speech it takes me a week; if I can talk as long as I want to it requires no preparation at all. I am ready now.

It reminds me of the famous quote attributed to a variety of great thinkers and writers: "If I had more time, I would have written a shorter letter."

So let's accept that creating a great talk to fit a limited time period is going to take real effort. But there's a right way and a wrong way to go about it.

THE WRONG WAY

The wrong way to condense your talk is to include all the things that you think you need to say, and simply cut them all back to make them a lot shorter. Funnily enough, you may well be able to create a script that achieves this. Every major topic you want to cover is there in summary form. Your work is covered! You may even think there's a throughline connecting it all, some broad underpinning of your work. To you it may feel like you've given it your all and done the best you can to fit the time you've been given to speak.

But throughlines that connect large numbers of concepts don't work. There's a drastic consequence when you rush through multiple topics in summary form. They don't land with any force. You know the full background and context to what you're saying, and so the insights you offer may seem profound to you. But for the audience, which is coming to your work fresh, the talk will probably come across as conceptual, dry, or superficial.

It's a simple equation. Overstuffed equals underexplained.

To say something interesting you have to take the time to do at least two things:

- Show why it matters . . . what's the question you're trying to answer, the problem you're trying to solve, the experience you're trying to share?
- Flesh out each point you make with real examples, stories, facts.

This is how ideas that you cherish can be built in someone else's mind. The trouble is that explaining the why and then giving the examples take time. And that leaves you with just one choice.

THE RIGHT WAY

To provide an effective talk, you must slash back the *range of topics* you will cover to a single, connected thread — a throughline that can be properly developed. In a sense, you cover less, but the impact will actually be significantly greater.

Author Richard Bach said, "Great writing is all about the power of the deleted word." It's true of speaking too. The secret of successful talks often lies in what is left out. Less can be more.

Many TED speakers have told us that this has been the key to getting their talk right. Here's musician Amanda Palmer.

I found my ego really trapping me. If my TED Talk goes viral, I need people to know what a great pianist I am! That I can also paint! That I write fantastic lyrics! That I have all these OTHER talents! THIS IS MY CHANCE! But, no. The only way the talk can truly soar is if you take your ego out of it and let yourself be a delivery vehicle for the ideas themselves. I remember going to dinner with TED regular Nicholas Negroponte and asked if he had any advice for my talk. He said something that my Buddhist-leaning mentor has been saying for years: leave space and SAY LESS.

Economist Nic Marks recommends the advice often given to fledgling writers: "*Kill your darlings*. I had to be prepared to NOT talk about some things I absolutely love and would have liked to squeeze in, but they were not part of the main narrative. That was tough but essential."

One of the most popular TED speakers, Brené Brown, also struggled to meet TED's tight time demands. She recommends this simple formula. "Plan your talk. Then cut it by half. Once you've grieved the loss of half of your talk, cut it another 50 percent. It's seductive to think about how much you can fit into 18 minutes. The better question for me is, 'What can you unpack *in a meaningful way* in 18 minutes?'"

This same issue applies to talks of any length. Let me try a personal example with you. Let's say I've been asked to speak for just 2 minutes to introduce who I am. Here's version 1:

Although I'm British, I was born in Pakistan — my father was a missionary eye surgeon — and my early years were spent there and in India and Afghanistan. At age thirteen, I was sent to boarding school in England, and after that I went to Oxford University for a degree in Philosophy, Politics, and Economics. I started work as a local newspaper journalist in Wales, then moved to a pirate radio station in the Seychelles Islands for a couple of years to write and read a world news service.

Back in the UK in the mid-1980s, I fell in love with computers and started a series of magazines devoted to them. It was a great time to be launching specialist magazines, and my company doubled in size every year for seven years. I sold it, moved to the US, and tried again.

By the year 2000 my business had grown to 2,000 employees and 150 magazines and websites. But the tech bubble was about to burst, and when it did, it nearly destroyed the company. Besides, who needs magazines when you have the Internet? I left at the end of 2001.

Happily, I had put some money into a nonprofit foundation that I was able to use to buy TED, which, back then, was an annual conference in California. That's been my full-time passion ever since.

And here's version 2:

I want you to come with me to a student's room at Oxford University in 1977. You open the door, and at first it seems like there's nobody there.

But wait. Over in the corner, there's a boy lying on the floor, face up, staring at the ceiling. He's been like that for more than 90 minutes. That's me. Twenty-year-old me. I am thinking. Hard. I am trying . . . please don't laugh . . . I am trying to solve the problem of free will. That deep mystery that has stumped the world's philosophers for at least two millennia? Yup, I'm taking it on.

Anyone looking objectively at the scene would have concluded that this boy was some weird combination of arrogant, deluded, or perhaps just socially awkward and lonely, preferring the company of ideas to people.

But my own narrative? I'm a dreamer. I've always been obsessed by the power of ideas. And I'm pretty sure it's that inward focus that helped me survive growing up in boarding schools in India and England, away from my missionary parents, and that gave me the confidence to try to build a media company. Certainly it was the dreamer in me that fell in love so deeply with TED.

Most recently I've been dreaming about the revolution in public speaking, and what it could lead to . . .

So which version tells you more about me? The first one certainly has far more facts. It's a decent summary of big parts of my life. A 2-minute resume. The second one focuses on just a single moment of my life. And yet, when I try this experiment on people, they say they find the second far more interesting, and also far more revealing.

Whether your time limit is 2 minutes, 18 minutes, or an hour, let's agree to this as a starting point: *You will only cover as much ground as you can dive into in sufficient depth to be compelling.*

And this is where the concept of a throughline really helps. By choosing a throughline you will automatically filter out much of what you might otherwise say. When I did the above experiment, I thought, *What aspect of me should I focus on for a little more depth?* The decision to go with "dreamer" made it easy to anchor version 2 on my time studying philosophy at Oxford and slash back most of the other parts of my life. If I had chosen "entrepreneur" or "nerd" or "global soul," I'd have made different cuts.

So a throughline requires you first to identify an idea that can be properly unpacked in the time you have available. You should then build a structure so that every element in your talk is somehow linked to this idea.

FROM THROUGHLINE TO STRUCTURE

Let's pause for a moment on that word *structure.* It's critical. Different talks can have very different structures tied onto that central throughline. A talk might begin with an introduction to the problem the speaker is tackling and give an anecdote that illustrates that problem. It might then move to some historical attempts to solve the problem and give two examples that ultimately failed. It could continue to the speaker's proposed solution, including one dramatic new piece of evidence that supports the idea. Then it might close with three implications for the future.

You can picture the structure of that talk as like a tree. There's a central throughline, rising vertically, with branches attached to it, each of which represents an expansion of the main narrative: one at the bottom for the opening anecdote; two just above that at the history section for the examples that failed; one at the proposed solution to mark the new evidence; and three at the top to illustrate the implications for the future.

Another talk might be simply sharing, one after the other, five pieces of work that have a connected theme, beginning and ending with the speaker's current project. In that structure you can think of the throughline as a loop that connects five different boxes, each representing one of the pieces of work.

The most viewed TED speaker at the time of writing this book is Sir Ken Robinson. He told me that most of his talks follow this simple structure:

A. Introduction — getting settled, what will be covered
B. Context — why this issue matters
C. Main Concepts
D. Practical Implications
E. Conclusion

He said, "There's an old formula for writing essays that says a good essay answers three questions: *What? So What? Now What?* It's a bit like that."

Of course, the appeal of Sir Ken's talks goes way beyond their structural simplicity, and neither he nor I would recommend that everyone adopt that same structure. What matters is that you find the structure that most powerfully develops your throughline in the time available, and that it is clear how each talk element ties into it.

TACKLING TOUGH TOPICS

Your throughline needs handling with special care if you have to speak on a heavy subject. The horror of a refugee crisis. The diabetes explosion. Gender-related violence in South America. Many speakers on these topics view their job as to highlight a cause that needs to be more widely known. The structure of these talks is typically to lay out a series of facts that illustrate how awful a situation is and why something must be done to fix it. And indeed there are times when that is the perfect way to frame a talk ... provided you're confident that your listeners are ready and willing to be made to feel uncomfortable.

The trouble is that if an audience sits through too many talks like this, it will get emotionally exhausted and will start to switch off. Compassion fatigue sets in. If that happens before your talk is done, you'll have no impact.

How can you route around that? The first step is to think of your talk not as being about an *issue,* but about an *idea.*

My former colleague June Cohen framed the difference this way:

An issue-based talk leads with *morality.* An idea-based talk leads with *curiosity.*

An issue exposes a *problem.* An idea proposes a *solution.*

An issue says, "Isn't this *terrible*?" An idea says, "Isn't this *interesting*?"

It's much easier to pull in an audience by framing the talk as an attempt to solve an intriguing riddle rather than as a plea for them to care. The first feels like a gift being offered. The second feels like an ask.

THE CHECKLIST

As you work on developing your throughline, here's a simple checklist:

- Is this a topic I'm passionate about?
- Does it inspire curiosity?
- Will it make a difference to the audience to have this knowledge?
- Is my talk a gift or an ask?
- Is the information fresh, or is it already out there?
- Can I truly explain the topic in the time slot allocated, complete with necessary examples?
- Do I know enough about this to make a talk worth the audience's time?
- Do I have the credibility to take on this topic?
- What are the fifteen words that encapsulate my talk?
- Would those fifteen words persuade someone they'd be interested in hearing my talk?

Speaking coach Abigail Tenembaum recommends testing your throughline on someone who could be a typical audience member, and to do so not in writing but verbally. "Saying it out loud often crystallizes for the speaker what is clear, what is missing, and how to sharpen it."

Best-selling author Elizabeth Gilbert also believes in planning a talk for an audience of one. She offered me this advice: "Choose a human being — an actual human being in your life — and prepare your talk as if you will be delivering it to that one person only. Choose someone who is not in your field, but who is generally an intelligent, curious, engaged, worldly person — and someone whom you really like. This will bring a warmth of spirit and heart to your talk. Most of all, be sure you are actually speaking to one person, and not to a demographic ('My speech is for people in the software field who are between the ages of twenty-two and thirty-eight.'), because a demographic is not a human being, and if you speak to a demographic, you will not sound like you are speaking to a human being. You don't have to go to their house and practice your talk on them for six months; they don't even need to know that you're doing this. Just choose your one ideal listener, and then do your best to create a talk that would blow their mind, or move them, or fascinate them, or delight them."

But most important of all, says Gilbert, is to pick a topic that lives deep within you. "Talk about what you know. Talk about what you know and love with all your heart. I want to hear about the subject that is most important to your life — not some random subject that you think will be a novelty. Bring me your well-worn passion of decades, not some fresh, radical gimmick, and trust me — I will be captivated."

Once you have your throughline, you're ready to plan what you'll attach to it. There are many ways to build ideas. Over the next five chapters we'll look at five core tools that speakers use:

- Connection
- Narration
- Explanation
- Persuasion
- Revelation

They can be mixed and matched. Some talks stick to a single tool. Others incorporate multiple elements. A few use all five (and often approximately in the order above). But it's worth looking at them separately because the five techniques are strikingly different.

Talk Tools

5

CONNECTION
Get Personal

Knowledge can't be pushed into a brain. It has to be pulled in.

Before you can build an idea in someone else's mind, you need their permission. People are naturally cautious about opening up their minds — the most precious thing they own — to complete strangers. You need to find a way to overcome that caution. And the way you do that is to make visible the human being cowering inside you.

Hearing a talk is a completely different thing from reading an essay. It's not just the words. Not at all. It's the person delivering the words. To make an impact, there has to be a human connection. You can give the most brilliant talk, with crystal-clear explanations and laser-sharp logic, but if you don't first connect with the audience, it just won't land. Even if the content is, at some level, understood, it won't be activated but simply filed away in some soon-to-be-forgotten mental archive.

People aren't computers. They're social creatures with all manner of ingenious quirks. They have evolved weapons to protect against dangerous knowledge polluting the worldview they depend on. Those weapons have names: skepticism, mistrust, dislike, boredom, incomprehension.

And, by the way, those weapons are invaluable. If your mind were open to all incoming language, your life would quickly fall apart. "Coffee gives you cancer!" "Those foreigners are disgusting!" "Buy these beautiful kitchen knives!" "I know how to give you a good time, baby . . ." Every single thing we see or hear is evaluated before we dare embed it into an actionable idea.

So your very first job as a speaker is to find a way to disarm those weapons and build a trusting human bond with the audience so that they're willing — delighted, even — to offer you full access to their minds for a few minutes.

If military metaphors aren't to your liking, let's go back to the idea of a talk as a journey. It is a journey you take your audience on. You may have figured out a brilliant route to a powerful destination. But before you can take people there, you have to make the journey seem enticing. Task one is to go to where the audience is and win them over. Yes, you're a guide who can be trusted. Without that, the whole endeavor may bog down before it has even started.

We tell our speakers that TED offers a warm, welcoming audience. But even so, there's a huge difference in impact between those speakers who connect and those who unconsciously trigger skepticism or boredom or dislike.

Happily, there are numerous ways to make that vital early connection. Here are five suggestions:

MAKE EYE CONTACT, RIGHT FROM THE START

Humans are good at forming instant judgments about other humans. Friend or foe. Likable or unlikable. Wise or dull. Confident or tentative. The clues we use to make these sweeping judgments are often shockingly light. The way someone dresses. How they walk, or stand. Their facial expression. Their body language. Their attentiveness.

Great speakers find a way of making an early connection with their audience. It can be as simple as walking confidently on stage, looking around, making eye contact with two or three people, and smiling. Take a look at the first few moments of Kelly McGonigal's TED Talk on the upside of stress. "I have a confession to make." *[she pauses, turns, drops hands, gives a little smile]* "But first, I want YOU to make a little confession to me." *[walks forward]* "In the past year" *[looks around intently from face to face]* "I want you to just raise your hand if you've experienced relatively little stress. Anyone?" *[an enigmatic smile, which a few moments later turns into a million-dollar smile]*. There is instant audience connection there.

Now, not all of us are as naturally fluent, relaxed, or beautiful as Kelly. But one thing we can all do is make eye contact with audience members and smile a little. It makes a huge difference. The Indian artist Raghava KK maintains great eye contact, as does Argentine democracy advocate Pia Mancini. Within seconds of them starting, you just feel yourself being reeled in.

There's a reason for this. Humans have evolved a sophisticated ability to read other people by looking at their eyes. We can subconsciously detect the tiniest movement of eye muscles in someone's face and use it to judge not just how they are feeling, but whether we can trust them. (And while we're doing that, they're doing the same to us.)

Scientists have shown that just the act of two people staring at each other will trigger mirror neuron activity that literally adopts the emotional state of the other person. If I'm beaming, I will make you smile inside. Just a bit. But a meaningful bit. If I'm nervous, you'll feel a little anxious too. We look at each other, and our minds sync.

And the extent to which our minds sync is determined in part by how much we instinctively trust each other. The best tool to engender that trust? Yup, a smile. A natural human smile. (People can detect fake smiles and immediately feel manipulated. Ron Gutman gave a TED Talk on the hidden power of smiles. It's well worth 7½ minutes of your time.)

Eye contact, backed by an occasional warm smile, is an amazing technology that can transform how a talk is received. (It's a shame, though, that it's sometimes undermined by another technology: stage lighting. Some lighting setups mean a speaker is dazzled by bright spotlights and can't even see the audience. Talk to the event organizer about this ahead of time. If you're on stage and feeling disconnected, it's OK to ask for the house lights to be raised or the stage lights dimmed a little.)

At TED, our number-one advice to speakers on the day of their talk is to make regular eye contact with members of the audience. Be warm. Be real. Be you. It opens the door to them trusting you, liking you, and beginning to share your passion.

When you walk onto the stage, you should be thinking about one thing: your true excitement at the chance to share your passion with the people sitting right there a few feet from you. Don't rush in with your opening sentence. Walk into the light, pick out a couple of people, look them in the eye, nod a greeting, and smile. Then you're on your way.

SHOW VULNERABILITY

One of the best ways to disarm an audience is to first reveal your own vulnerability. It's the equivalent of the tough cowboy walking into a saloon and holding his coat wide open to reveal no weapons. Everyone relaxes.

Brené Brown gave a wonderful talk on vulnerability at TEDx-Houston, and she began it appropriately.

A couple years ago, an event planner called me because I was going to do a speaking event. And she said, "I'm really struggling with how to write about you on the little flyer." And I thought, "Well, what's the struggle?" And she said, "Well, I saw you speak, and I'm going to call you a researcher, I think, but I'm afraid if I call you a researcher, no one will come, because they'll think you're boring and irrelevant."

You love her already.

By the same logic, if you're feeling nervous, it can actually work in your favor. Audiences sense it instantly and — far from despising you as you may fear, the opposite happens — they begin rooting for you. We often encourage speakers who look like they may struggle with nerves to simply be ready, if necessary, to acknowledge it. If you feel yourself choking up, then pause . . . pick up a bottle of water, take a sip, and just say what you're feeling. "Hang in there a moment . . . As you can see, I'm feeling a little nervous here. Normal service will be restored soon." Likely as not, you'll get a warm round of applause, and a crowd dying for you to succeed.

Vulnerability can be powerful at any stage of a talk. One of the most stunning moments witnessed on the TED stage came when neurosurgeon and best-selling author Sherwin Nuland had just completed a tour-de-force history of electroshock therapy, the treatment for severe mental illness that involves sending electric current directly through a patient's brain. He was knowledgeable and funny, and he made it all seem interesting, if a little terrifying. But then he stopped. "Why am I telling you this story at this meeting?" He said he wanted to share something he'd never spoken or written about before. You could have heard a pin drop.

"The reason . . . is that I am a man who, almost thirty years ago, had his life saved by two long courses of electroshock therapy." Nuland went on to unveil his own secret history of debilitating depression, an illness that got so bad doctors were planning to remove part of his brain. Instead, as a last resort, they tried electroshock therapy. And eventually, after twenty treatments, it had worked.

By making himself so deeply vulnerable to the audience, he was able to end his talk with extraordinary power.

> I've always felt that somehow I was an impostor because my readers don't know what I have just told you. So one of the reasons that I have come here to talk about this today is to — frankly, selfishly — unburden myself and let it be known that this is not an untroubled mind that has written all of these books. But more importantly, I think, is the fact that a very significant proportion of people in this audience are under thirty and it looks to me like almost all of you are on the cusp of a magnificent and exciting career. Anything can happen to you. Things change. Accidents happen. Something from childhood comes back to haunt you. You can be thrown off the track . . . If I can find my way back from this, believe me, anybody can find their way back from any adversity that exists in their lives. And for those who are older, who have lived through difficult times, perhaps where they lost everything, as I did, and started out all over again, some of these things will seem very familiar. There is recovery. There is redemption. And there is resurrection.

This is a talk everyone should see. Sherwin Nuland passed away in 2014, but his vulnerability, and consequent inspiration, live on.

Willing to be vulnerable is one of the most powerful tools a speaker can wield. But as with anything powerful, it should be handled with care. Brené Brown has seen a lot of speakers misinterpret her advice. She told me: "Formulaic or contrived personal sharing leaves audiences feeling manipulated and often hostile toward you and your message. Vulnerability is not oversharing. There's a simple equation: vulnerability minus boundaries is not vulnerability. It can be anything from an attempt to hotwire connection to attention-seeking, but it's not vulnerability and it doesn't lead to connection. The best way I've found to get clear on this is to really examine our intentions. Is sharing done in service of the work on stage or is it a way to work through our own stuff? The former is powerful, the latter damages the confidence people have in us."

Brown strongly recommends that you *don't* share parts of yourself that you haven't yet worked through.

"We need to have owned our stories before sharing them is experienced as a gift. A story is only ready to share when the presenter's healing and growth is not dependent on the audience's response to it."

Authentic vulnerability is powerful. Oversharing is not. If in doubt, try your talk on an honest friend.

MAKE 'EM LAUGH — BUT NOT SQUIRM!

Concentrating on a talk can be hard work, and humor is a wonderful way to bring the audience with you. If Sophie Scott is right, part of the evolutionary purpose of laughter is to create social bonding. When you laugh with someone, you both feel you're on the same side. It's a fantastic tool for building a connection.

Indeed, for many great speakers, humor has become a super-weapon. Sir Ken Robinson's talk on schools' failure to nurture creativity, which as of 2015 had powered its way to 35 million views on TED, was given on the final day of the conference. He started like this. "It's been great, hasn't it? I've been blown away. In fact, I'm leaving." The audience giggled. And basically never stopped. From that moment, he owned us. Humor hacks away the main resistance to listening to a talk. By offering little gifts of

laughter from the start, you are subtly informing your audience
... *Come along for the ride, dear friends. It's going to be a treat.*

Audiences who laugh with you quickly come to like you. And
if people like you, they're much readier to take seriously what you
have to say. Laughter blows open someone's defenses, and suddenly you have a chance to truly communicate with them.

There's another big benefit of laughter early in a talk. It's a
powerful signal that you're connecting. Monica Lewinsky told
me that the moment her nervousness went away during her TED
Talk was when the audience erupted with laughter. And if it's
a signal to the speaker, it's also a signal to everyone else in the
room. Laughter says, *We as a group have bonded with this speaker.*
Everyone then pays more attention.

It's striking that some of the very best speakers spend a significant portion of their talks building this connection. In Sir Ken's
case above, almost all of the first 11 minutes is a series of hilarious education-related stories that do little to advance his main
idea, but instead create an extraordinary bond with the audience.
We're thinking: *This is SO much fun. I never thought education
could be such an engaging topic. You are such an appealing person
... I'd go with you anywhere.* And when he eventually gets serious and moves into his main point about the loss of creativity in
schools, we're hanging on every word.

Likewise, in Bryan Stevenson's spellbinding talk about injustice, he spent the first quarter of his time on a single story
about how his grandmother had persuaded him never to drink.
The story ended hilariously, and suddenly we all felt deeply connected to this man.

Caution: Successfully spending that much time on humorous
stories is a special gift, not recommended for most of us. But if
you can find just one short story that makes people smile, it may
unlock the rest of your talk.

Comic sci-fi author Rob Reid offered a very different type of humor: satire. His tone throughout was serious. He claimed to be offering a sober analysis of "copyright math." But after a minute or so, people began realizing that actually he was mocking the absurdity of copyright laws that regarded every illegally down-loaded song as the equivalent of stealing $150,000. The giggles started and quickly flared into guffaws.

Of course, it doesn't always work. One speaker at TED a few years ago clearly thought he was being hilarious in telling a series of ever more awkward stories about his ex-wife. Maybe a couple of friends in the audience were chuckling. The rest of us were cringing. On another occasion, a speaker tried to perform ev-ery quotation in his talk in the accent he imagined the author of the quote might have had. Perhaps his family found this to be endearing. On a public stage, it was just embarrassing. (Unless you're extremely talented, I strongly recommend avoiding ac-cents, other than your own!)

Thirty years ago, speakers packed their talks with jokes based on gender, race, and disability. Don't go there! The world has changed.

Humor is a skilled art, and not everyone can do it. Ineffec-tive humor is worse than no humor at all. Telling a joke that you downloaded off the Internet will probably backfire. Indeed jokes per se seem hackneyed, clumsy, and unsophisticated. What you're looking for instead are hilarious-but-true stories that are directly relevant to your topic or are an endearing, humorous use of language.

The funniest person on our team is Tom Rielly, who runs our fellows program and for years gave a final wrap-up of the confer-ence that skewered every speaker with wicked hilarity. Here's his advice:

1. Tell anecdotes relevant to your subject matter, where humor is natural. The best humor is based on observation

of things occurring around you and then exaggerating or remixing them.

2. Have a funny remark ready if you flub your words, the A/V goes awry, or if the clicker doesn't work. The audience has been there and you instantly win their sympathy.

3. Build humor into your visuals. You can also have the humor be the contrast between what you're saying and what you're showing. There are lots of great possibilities for laughter.

4. Use satire, saying the opposite of what you mean, then revealing your intent, though this is really hard to get right.

5. Timing is critical. If there's a laughter moment, you have to give it a chance to land. That may take the courage to pause just for a moment. And to do so without it looking like you're fishing for applause.

6. Very important: If you're not funny, don't try to be funny. Test the humor on family or friends, or even a colleague. Are they laughing? If not, change it or spike it.

Dangers (even in the hands of people blessed with the gift of humor):

1. Off-color remarks and offensive language: Don't. You're not speaking at a late-night comedy club.

2. Limericks or other seemingly funny poetry

3. Puns

4. Sarcasm

5. Going on too long

6. Any attempted humor based on religion, ethnicity, gender identity, politics. Members of those communities maybe can; outsiders definitely can't.

All of these can work in the right circumstances but are fraught with the possibility of bombing or causing offense. If the audience experiences either, it's hard to get them back.

If you plan to do a lot of public speaking, it's really worth trying to find your own brand of humor that works. And if not, don't panic. It's not for everyone. There are plenty of other ways to connect.

PARK YOUR EGO

Would you want to trust your mind to someone who was completely full of himself? Nothing damages the prospects of a talk more than the sense that the speaker is a blowhard. And if that happens early on . . . look out.

I vividly remember a TED Talk from many years ago that began: "Before I became a living brand . . ." And there, right there, you knew it wasn't going to end well. The speaker was on a high after some recent major commercial success, and we were going to hear about every last bit of it. That's the only time at TED I remember a talk being interrupted by hisses. *Hisses!* Even if you truly are a genius, a drop-dead-gorgeous athlete, and a fearless leader, it's best to let your audience figure that out for themselves.

TED speaker Salman Khan put it beautifully:

> Be yourself. The worst talks are the ones where someone is trying to be someone they aren't. If you are generally goofy, then be goofy. If you are emotional, then be emotional. The one exception to that is if you are arrogant and self-centered. Then you should definitely pretend to be someone else.

Some speakers use humor to land a deliberate blow to their egos.

Dan Pink, an accomplished speaker whose talk on motivation

has 10 million views and counting, walked onto the stage looking just a bit overconfident and began speaking in a voice that was just a tad too loud. But after his first few sentences, we were all in his pocket. This is what he said:

> I need to make a confession at the outset here. A little over twenty years ago I did something that I regret, something that I'm not particularly proud of, something that, in many ways, I wish no one would ever know, but here I feel kind of obliged to reveal. In the late 1980s, in a moment of youthful indiscretion, I went to law school.

Brilliant. Now we liked him after all.

Self-deprecation, in the right hands, is a beautiful thing. Tony Blair is a master at it, often using self-deprecation to win over potentially hostile audiences. Once, before he was elected British prime minister, he began to tell a story which, he said apologetically, might make people worry whether he was qualified to govern. He told of a visit to the Netherlands, where, at a meal with dignitaries, he encountered a well-dressed woman in her fifties. She asked him who he was. "Tony Blair." "And what do you do?" "I lead the British Labour Party." He asked her who she was. "Beatrix." "And what do you do?" *[awkward pause]* "I'm the queen." Another speaker would have just name-dropped that he'd had dinner with the Queen of the Netherlands and lost the audience before he started. By deliberately talking himself down, Blair won laughter, affection, and trust.

Ego emerges in lots of ways that may be truly invisible to a speaker who's used to being the center of attention:

- Name-dropping
- Stories that seem designed only to show off
- Boasting about your or your company's achievements

- Making the talk all about you rather than an idea others can use.

I could tell you to go back to basics and to remember that the purpose of your talk is to gift an idea, not to self-promote. But even then you might miss it. It can be hard to see from the inside. Every leader needs someone she can count on for raw, honest feedback. Someone who's not afraid to upset or offend if need be. If you're feeling proud of what you've recently accomplished, it's important to try out your talk on that trusted person, and then give them the chance to say, "That was great in parts. But honestly? You come over a little full of yourself."

TELL A STORY

Storytelling is so important that the entire next chapter is dedicated to it, but one of its most important functions is to build connection with the audience.

We're born to love stories. They are instant generators of interest, empathy, emotion, and intrigue. They can brilliantly establish the context of a talk and make people care about a topic.

Powerful stories can appear at any stage of a talk. A great way to open. A great way to illustrate in the middle. And sometimes, though less often, a great way to end.

Ernesto Sirolli wanted to give a talk about a better approach to development aid in Africa. If you're going to take on a tough subject like that, it's a very good idea to connect with the audience first. Here's how he did it.

Our first project . . . was where we Italians decided to teach Zambian people how to grow food. So we arrived there with

Italian seeds in southern Zambia in this absolutely magnificent valley going down to the Zambezi River, and we taught the local people how to grow Italian tomatoes and zucchini and . . . And of course the local people had absolutely no interest in doing that . . . And we were amazed that the local people, in such a fertile valley, would not have any agriculture. But instead of asking them how come they were not growing anything, we simply said, "Thank God we're here. Just in the nick of time to save the Zambian people from starvation." And of course, everything in Africa grew beautifully. We had these magnificent tomatoes . . . And we could not believe, and we were telling the Zambians, "Look how easy agriculture is." When the tomatoes were nice and ripe and red, overnight, some two hundred hippos came out from the river and they ate everything. And we said to the Zambians, "My God, the hippos!" And the Zambians said, "Yes, that's why we have no agriculture here."

When you can pull together humor, self-deprecation, and insight into a single story, you have yourself a winning start.

The stories that can generate the best connection are stories about you personally or about people close to you. Tales of failure, awkwardness, misfortune, danger, or disaster, told authentically, are often the moment when listeners shift from plain vanilla interest to deep engagement. They have started to share some of your emotions. They have started to care about you. They have started to like you.

But be careful. Some stories can come over as boastful or emotionally manipulative. When you explain the amazing way you turned a problem into a thrilling success, far from connecting, you may actually turn people off. When you pull the photograph of your eldest son from your jacket pocket right at the end of your talk, declare that he's been diagnosed with a terminal illness, and say that your talk is devoted to him, you may make your audience more uncomfortable than sympathetic.

The guideline here is just to be authentic. Is that the real you telling this story? A good test is to imagine whether you would tell this story to a group of old friends. And if so, how. Friends are good detectors of the inauthentic. And so are audiences. Be real, and you won't go too far wrong.

And that advice applies to this entire chapter on connection. I've sometimes described these suggestions as tools or techniques. It's important they don't come over that way. They need to be part of an authentic desire to connect. You're a human. Your listeners are humans. Think of them as friends. And just reach out.

AH, POLITICS

I can't end this chapter without lamenting the biggest killer of connection: tribal thinking. Whether in politics, religion, or race, people who are part of a community that has rejected wholesale the ideas you want to articulate, are, to say the least, a challenging audience.

Did my reference above to Tony Blair make you angry at me? After years in power, and especially because of his support for the war in Iraq, he became hated by some to the point where just mentioning his name raised their stress levels. For them, the example above will have seemed poorly chosen. Its explanatory purpose will have been ignored.

Politics can do this. And so can religion. Some views are held so deeply that if a speaker seems to be threatening them, people go into a different mode. Instead of listening, they shut down and smolder.

This is a very big problem. One of the most consequential pieces of public speaking in recent times has been the presentation Al Gore began making in 2005 that was turned into the documentary *An Inconvenient Truth,* proclaiming a global climate crisis. He made powerful use of every talk technique you can imagine: compelling slides, careful logic, eloquence, humor, passionate advocacy, devastating mockery of opposing views, and even a touching personal story about his daughter. When he gave the presentation at a special off-the-record session of TED, it profoundly impacted the lives of many participants, persuading some to chuck in their jobs and work full-time on climate issues.

There was one problem, though. Al Gore was a politician in a country sharply divided on partisan lines. Our partisan instincts build near-impregnable barriers against propaganda from the other side. Half of the country connected more deeply with Gore than ever, embraced *An Inconvenient Truth,* and had their worldviews permanently altered. The other half never connected at all. They simply shut it out. The very fact that it was Gore the politician making the case meant that it couldn't be true. A decade later, the climate issue was as politicized as ever. What should be a matter of science had tragically become a test of political alignment. (It's possible the same thing would have happened on the left if Dick Cheney or Karl Rove had led the charge on a major global issue.)

The toxicity of our political (and religious) nonconversations is a true tragedy of the modern world. When people aren't prepared or ready to listen, communication can't happen.

If you want to reach people who radically disagree with you, your only chance is to put yourself in their shoes as best you can. Don't use language that may trigger tribal responses. Start with a vision of the world as seen through *their* eyes. And use every one of the tools described here to build a connection based on your shared humanity.

Happily, most speaking opportunities are with fundamentally welcoming audiences. You should readily be able to make a connection with them. And then your talk can truly shine.

6

NARRATION

The Irresistible Allure of Stories

Stories helped make us who we are. I mean this literally. The best evidence from archaeology and anthropology suggests that the human mind coevolved with storytelling.

About a million years ago, our hominid ancestors began gaining control of the use of fire, and it seems to have had a profound impact on their development. Warmth, yes. Defense against predators, yes. Cooking and its remarkable consequences for the growth of our brains, yes. But there was something else.

Fire created a new magnet for social bonding. Its warmth and flickering light drew people together after dark. This seems to have happened in every ancient hunter-gatherer culture over the last three hundred thousand years.

And what did they do with this time together? It seems that, in many cultures, one form of social interaction became prevalent: storytelling.

Anthropologist Polly Wiessner has spent forty years researching certain forager cultures and periodically recording who said what and when. In 2014, she published a paper that showed a dramatic difference between daytime and nighttime gatherings. Daytime talk, even when larger groups were involved, centered on economic discussions and social gossip. At night, the mood mellowed. There might be singing, dancing, rituals. But the most time was spent on storytelling. Tales that brought people from distant places to the hearth and into the hearts and minds of listeners. Tales of people alive and dead. Present and distant. Tales evoking hilarity, tension, and awe. Tales told by men. Tales told by women. Often the star storytellers were elders. In some cases, they had lost their sight but were still venerated for their oral storytelling.

Professor Wiessner told me that these stories played a crucial role in helping expand people's ability to imagine and dream and understand the minds of others. They allowed human minds to explore vast social networks and to build imagined communities far beyond the borders of their local social group. Stories brought social status to great storytellers and actionable insights to great listeners. (For example, an attentive listener could learn how to avoid the life-threatening dangers described in a story.) Therefore, those narrating and listening skills are likely to have been selected for as modern humans evolved.

So it's not just that we all love hearing stories. They probably helped shape how our minds share and receive information.

Certainly, the power of stories has continued to this day, as evidenced by the multi-billion-dollar industries built around novels, movies, and TV.

And it's no surprise to discover that many of the best talks are anchored in storytelling. Unlike challenging explanations or complex arguments, everyone can relate to stories. They typically have a simple linear structure that makes them easy to follow. You just let the speaker take you on a journey, one step at a time. Thanks to our long history around campfires, our minds are really good at tracking along.

And a natural part of listening to stories is that you empathize with the experiences of the characters. You find yourself immersed in their thoughts and emotions. In fact, you physically feel what they feel; if they're stressed or excited or exhilarated, so are you. And that makes you care about the outcome. Your attention is held.

What are the elements of a great story? The classic formula is: A protagonist with goals meets an unexpected obstacle and a crisis results. The protagonist attempts to overcome the obstacle, leading to a climax, and finally a denouement. (There can also be interruptions and plot twists.)

When it comes to sharing a story from the stage, remember to emphasize four key things:

- Base it on a character your audience can empathize with.
- Build tension, whether through curiosity, social intrigue, or actual danger.
- Offer the right level of detail. Too little and the story is not vivid. Too much and it gets bogged down.
- End with a satisfying resolution, whether funny, moving, or revealing.

Of course, it's all in the execution, so it's really worth fine-tuning your stories. Often, especially with stories from our own lives, we overstuff with details that are important to us, but that a wider audience just doesn't need to know. Or, worse, we forget an essential piece of context, without which the story doesn't make much sense.

Here's a great story:

Once, when I was eight years old, my father took me fishing. We were in a tiny boat, five miles from shore, when a massive storm blew in. Dad put a life jacket on me and whispered in my ear, "Do you trust me, son?" I nodded. He threw me overboard. *[pause]* I kid you not. Just tossed me over! I hit the water and bobbed up to the surface, gasping for breath. It was shockingly cold. The waves were terrifying. Monstrous. Then . . . Dad dived in after me. We watched in horror as our little boat flipped and sank. But he was holding me the whole time, telling me it was going to be OK. Fifteen minutes later, the Coast Guard helicopter arrived. It turned out that Dad knew the boat was damaged and was going to sink, and he had called them with our exact location. He guessed it was better to chuck me in the open sea than risk getting trapped when the boat flipped. And that is how I learned the true meaning of the word trust.

And here's how not to tell it:

I learned trust from my father when I was eight years old and we got caught in a storm while out fishing for mackerel. We failed to catch a single one before the storm hit. Dad knew the boat was going to sink, because it was one of those Saturn brand inflatable boats, which are usually pretty strong, but this one had been punctured once and Dad thought it might happen again. In any case, the storm was too big for an inflatable boat and it was already leaking. So he called the Coast Guard rescue service, who, back then, were available 24/7, unlike today. He told them our location, and then, to avoid the risk of getting trapped underwater, he put a life jacket on me and threw me overboard before jumping in himself. We then waited for the Coast Guard to come and, sure enough, 15 minutes later the helicopter showed up — I think it was a Sikorsky MH-60 Jayhawk — and we were fine.

The first story has a character you care about and intense drama that builds to incredulity before being beautifully resolved. The second version is a mess. The drama is killed by revealing the father's intent too early; there's no attempt to share the actual experience of the kid; there are too many details included that are irrelevant to most of the audience, while other germane details like the giant waves are ignored. Worst of all, the key line that anchors the story, "Do you trust me, son?," is lost. If you're going to tell a story, make sure you know *why* you're telling it, and try to edit out all the details that are not needed to make your point, while still leaving enough in for people to vividly imagine what happened.

Some of the greatest talks are built around a single story. This structure offers the speaker huge benefits:

- The throughline is taken care of. (It is simply the narrative arc of the story.)
- Provided the story is compelling, you can evoke an intense response in the audience.
- If the story is about you, you will create empathy for some of the things you care most about.
- It's easy to remember what you're going to say because the structure is linear, and your brain is extremely comfortable recalling one event right after another.

Many speakers therefore use a speaking slot simply to share their own story. It is the simplest, easiest-to-prepare type of talk there is. And there's a comfort to it. You *know* your story. You certainly know more about it than anyone in the audience.

If your journey has been remarkable, and if there's a coherence to the narrative, this type of talk can work really well.

But there's a trap here too. Remember, the goal is to give. Personal stories sometimes fail to do that. They may entertain or intrigue or boost the speaker's ego. But they don't automatically give the audience something they can walk away with: Insights, actionable information, perspective, context, hope.

And that's a real shame. One of the biggest reasons we turn down applications to speak at TED is when we're offered compelling anecdotes but no central idea that wraps the narrative together. This is heartbreaking, because the speakers are often wonderful, fascinating people. But without the wraparound of an idea, it's an opportunity missed.

The key shift needed is an artful edit of your journey that links together critical moments in a way that someone else can derive meaning from them. Without that, even if your life has been impressive, the talk may feel rambling and self-indulgent. But if the journey reveals something powerful you have learned, and if each step in your journey is revealed with humility and honesty and vulnerability, it is a journey we will gladly make with you.

There's one other nonnegotiable essential if you're to tell your own story. *It has to be true.* This may seem obvious, but, alas, speakers are sometimes tempted to exaggerate or even fabricate. Precisely because a story can have so much impact, they want to cast themselves or their organizations in the best possible light, and they sometimes cross that line called *truth.* Doing this is the easiest way to destroy your reputation. When talks go public, there may be thousands of eyes watching them. It only takes one person to notice that something's not quite right, and you can find yourself in hot water. It's not worth the risk.

When you combine a truthful story with a desire to use it for others' benefit, you can give your listeners an extraordinary gift.

Psychologist Eleanor Longden was willing to share publicly how at university she began hearing voices in her head, and how that led to her being diagnosed with schizophrenia, institutionalized, and driven to the point of suicide. The story alone is riveting, but she builds it so that you leave the talk with inspiring insights on schizophrenia, mental illness, and how we might rethink our responses to them. Here's part of the ending:

> There is no greater honor or privilege than facilitating that process of healing for someone; to bear witness, to reach out a hand, to share the burden of someone's suffering, and to hold the hope for their recovery. And likewise, for survivors of distress and adversity, that we don't have to live our lives forever defined by the

damaging things that have happened to us. We are unique. We are irreplaceable. What lies within us can never be truly colonized, contorted, or taken away. The light never goes out.

Explorer Ben Saunders went on a trek to the South Pole that almost took his life. He's a powerful storyteller and has great photographs to illustrate what happened. As he drew near the end of his talk, we waited expectantly for the usual admonitions adventurers offer us to go out and discover our true selves in whatever challenge we take on. But Ben surprised us. He shared some dark moments he'd experienced since the trek and said the destination he'd been dreaming of for years was less satisfying than the journey. The takeaway? Don't pin your happiness on the future.

> If we can't feel content here, today, now, on our journeys, amidst the mess and the striving that we all inhabit, the open loops, the half-finished to-do lists, the could-do-better-next-times, then we might never feel it.

Writer Andrew Solomon described how he was humiliated as a child, even before he came out as gay, and turned the story into an exhilarating essay on identity that anyone could relate to and learn from.

> There's always somebody who wants to confiscate our humanity, and there are always stories that restore it. If we live out loud, we can trounce the hatred and expand everyone's lives.

Sir Ken Robinson's hilarious celebration of the importance of creativity in children is anchored in a story. He describes how a doctor in the 1930s noticed that a young girl who was failing at school had an irresistible desire to dance. Instead of medicating her, he persuaded her mother to send her to dance school. The girl was Gillian Lynne, who became the hugely successful choreographer for Andrew Lloyd Webber. This story, told in Sir Ken's inimitable style, is a moving illustration of the perils and potential in how schools handle creativity, and it is the part of the talk that turns hilarity into inspiration.

THE POWER OF PARABLE

Some stories are carefully designed as metaphors. There's a useful word for this type of story: *parable.*

Traditionally, a parable is a story that carries a moral or spiritual lesson. It's a tool that's been used by religious teachers throughout history to great effect. The stories of Jesus, I think we can agree, have clocked up even more views than Sir Ken's. But we can extend the word's meaning to cover any story that carries with it the power of metaphor.

Law professor Lawrence Lessig is a brilliant purveyor of parables. He came to TED in 2013 to argue that America's political process had become irredeemably corrupted by money. He had us imagine a foolish country called Lesterland in which only the people named Lester were able to vote. Clearly that would be ridiculous. But then he pointed out that the number of people named Lester in the US is about the same as the number of significant political funders. And that members of Congress have their priorities largely set by those funders, so that effectively it's only the funders whose views and votes matter. In this parable, we all live in Lesterland.

Writer Malcolm Gladwell also specializes in parables — and the appeal of this form is reflected in the amazing sales of his books and the high number of views on his TED Talks. His most popular talk is, believe it or not, a tale about the development of new forms of spaghetti sauce. But he uses it as a parable for the insight that different people want very different things but often don't have the language to say what they want, until you find the right questions to ask them.

What's satisfying about each of these talks is the way they draw out the meaning from the story. You don't want to insult the intelligence of the audience by force-feeding exactly the conclusion they must draw from the tale you've told. But you absolutely do want to be sure there's enough there for your listeners to be able to connect the dots. And this is where knowing your audience well is important. A parable might work very well with an audience that already knows your field, but it will need much greater elucidation for those outside it. It's important to test your material on someone who knows the audience to see if it lands with clarity but without clumsiness.

There are plenty of other risks in going the parable route. Sometimes the analogy doesn't quite fit. It can mislead as much as enlighten. Or you can spend so much time telling the story that you miss drawing out the necessary conclusions. But in the right hands, a parable can entertain, inform, and inspire all in one.

There is another powerful function that stories offer: Explanation. For this purpose they aren't usually the main attraction, but more the support. And they usually come in the form of short inserts designed to illustrate or reinforce an idea. We'll dig into this use of stories in the next chapter.

Meanwhile, remember this: Stories resonate deeply in every human. By giving your talk as a story or a series of related stories, you can greatly increase your connection with your listeners. But, please: let it mean something.

7

EXPLANATION

How to Explain Tough Concepts

Harvard psychologist Dan Gilbert came to TED with a daunting task. In just a single short talk, he planned to explain a sophisticated concept called "synthesized happiness" and why it led us to make wildly inaccurate predictions about our own futures.

Let's see how he set about it. Here's how he begins:

> When you have 21 minutes to speak, two million years seems like a really long time.

An opening line anchored in the here and now, but immediately creating intrigue.

> But evolutionarily, two million years is nothing. And yet in two million years, the human brain has nearly tripled in mass, going from the one-and-a-quarter-pound brain of our ancestor here, *[Homo] habilis,* to the almost three-pound meatloaf that everybody here has between their ears. What is it about a big brain that nature was so eager for every one of us to have one?

Do you feel a little spark of curiosity? That's the first step to a successful explanation. Once a mind is intrigued, it opens up. It *wants* new ideas.

Gilbert continues to tease:

> Well, it turns out when brains triple in size, they don't just get three times bigger; they gain new structures. And one of the main reasons our brain got so big is because it got a new part,

called . . . the prefrontal cortex. What does a prefrontal cortex do for you that should justify the entire architectural overhaul of the human skull in the blink of evolutionary time?

While continuing to stoke our curiosity, Gilbert just slotted in the first concept he'll be building on: *prefrontal cortex.*

One of the most important things it does: it's an experience simulator. Pilots practice in flight simulators so that they don't make real mistakes in planes. Human beings have this marvelous adaptation that they can actually have experiences in their heads before they try them out in real life. This is a trick that none of our ancestors could do, and that no other animal can do quite like we can. It's a marvelous adaptation. It's up there with opposable thumbs and standing upright and language as one of the things that got our species out of the trees and into the shopping mall.

Slipped in along with the humor, we get another cool new concept. *Experience simulator.* That's a key building block. It was dropped into place courtesy of a simple metaphor, the flight simulator. We already know what that is, so it's possible to imagine what an experience simulator might be. But could it be made clearer with an example? Yes, it could:

Ben and Jerry's doesn't have liver-and-onion ice cream, and it's not because they whipped some up, tried it, and went, yuck. It's because, without leaving your armchair, you can simulate that flavor and say yuck before you make it.

A single vivid example of the simulator in action, and you totally get it. But now the talk takes an intriguing twist.

Let's see how your experience simulators are working. Let's just run a quick diagnostic before I proceed with the rest of the talk.

Here are two different futures that I invite you to contemplate. You can try to simulate them and tell me which one you think you might prefer. One of them is winning the lottery. And the other is becoming paraplegic.

The audience is laughing, but a little nervously, wondering what's to come. And what's to come is a truly astonishing slide. Gilbert shows us data suggesting that, one year after winning the lottery or becoming a paraplegic, both groups are actually *equally happy*. What?! That can't be right. This cool new concept of the experience simulator has suddenly taken you to a place you didn't expect. A baffling place. The facts you're presented with make no sense. You're experiencing a *knowledge gap* and your mind is craving that it be filled.

So Gilbert proceeds to fill it, by offering another new concept.

The research that my laboratory has been doing . . . has revealed something really quite startling to us, something we call the impact bias, which is the tendency for the simulator to work badly . . . to make you believe that different outcomes are more different than in fact they really are.

By putting a name on it — *impact bias* — the mystery somehow becomes more believable. But our curiosity is burning more brightly than ever in its attempt to bridge this gap. Can it really be the case that we could mispredict our future happiness levels to this degree? Gilbert taps into that vein of curiosity to unveil his key concept.

From field studies to laboratory studies, we see that winning or losing an election, gaining or losing a romantic partner, getting or not getting a promotion, passing or not passing a college test, on and on, have far less impact, less intensity, and much less duration than people expect them to have. This al-

most floors me — a recent study showing how major life trau-
mas affect people suggests that, if it happened over three
months ago, with only a few exceptions, it has no impact
whatsoever on your happiness.

Why? Because happiness can be synthesized! . . . Human beings have something that we might think of as a psychological immune system. A system of cognitive processes, largely
nonconscious cognitive processes, that help them change their
views of the world so that they can feel better about the worlds
in which they find themselves.

There it is, *synthetic happiness* explained. It's been built on the
concepts of *prefrontal cortex, experience simulator,* and *impact
bias.* And to make it clear, Gilbert uses another metaphor, that
of the *immune system.* You already know what an immune system is, so to think of this as a *psychological* immune system is
easy. The concept is not delivered in a single leap but piece by
piece, and with metaphors to guide and show how the pieces fit
together.

But perhaps we're still not fully believing it. So Gilbert encourages us that he really does mean what he seems to be saying by
giving a series of examples of people's psychological immune sys-
tems at work:

- A disgraced politician who is grateful for his fall,
- A falsely convicted inmate who describes his thirty-seven
  years in jail as "a glorious experience,"
- And Pete Best, the Fab Four's rejected drummer, who fa-
  mously said, "I'm happier than I would have been with the
  Beatles."

The examples really drive his point home. Gilbert goes on to
show how this phenomenon can be observed everywhere, and

how you can live a wiser, happier life if you take it into account. After all, why do we chase happiness when we have the capacity within ourselves to manufacture the very commodity we crave?

But already we've seen enough to reveal the core elements of a masterful explanation. Let's recap:

Step 1. He started right where we were. Both literally, "When you have 21 minutes to speak . . . ," and conceptually, without daunting assumptions about our knowledge of psychology or neuroscience.

Step 2. He lit a fire called *curiosity*. Curiosity is what makes people ask *why?* and *how?* It's the feeling that something doesn't quite make sense. That there's a knowledge gap that has to be closed. This happened right at the start and then was dialed up dramatically with his unexpected data about paraplegics and lottery winners.

Step 3. He brought in concepts one by one. You can't understand the main concept without first being introduced to the pieces on which it depends, in this case prefrontal cortex, experience simulator, and impact bias.

Step 4. He used metaphors. It took metaphors like the flight simulator and the psychological immune system to make clear what he was talking about. For an explanation to be satisfying it has to take puzzling facts and build a connection from them to someone's *existing* mental model of the world. Metaphors and analogies are the key tools needed to do this. They help shape the explanation until finally it snaps into place with a satisfying *aha!*

Step 5. He used examples. Little stories, like that of Pete Best, help lock the explanation into place. This is like saying to the brain: *You think you understand this idea? Then apply it to these facts. If it fits, you've got this figured out.*

At the end of his explanation, our mental model of the world has been upgraded. It's richer, deeper, truer. A better reflection of reality.

Explanation is the act that consciously adds a new element to someone's mental model or reorders existing elements in a more satisfying way. If, as I have suggested, the goal of a great talk is to build an idea inside someone's mind, then explanation is the essential tool for achieving that goal.

Many of the best TED Talks achieve their greatness through masterful explanation. And there's a beautiful word for the gift they give: *Understanding*. We can define it as the upgrading of a worldview to better reflect reality.

There is evidence from numerous diverse sources, from neuroscience to psychology to educational theory, that this is how understanding must happen. It's built as a hierarchy, with each layer supplying the elements that construct the next layer. We start with what we know, and we add bits piece by piece, with each part positioned by using already understood language, backed by metaphors and examples. The metaphors, perhaps literally, reveal the "shape" of the new concept so that the mind knows how to slot it in effectively. Without this shaping, the concepts can't be put in place, so a key part of planning a talk is to have the balance right between the concepts you are introducing and the examples and metaphors needed to make them understandable.

Lexicographer Erin McKean offers this as a nice example of the power of metaphor.

If you were giving a talk about JavaScript to a general audience, you could explain that people often have a mental model of a computer program as being a set of instructions, executed one after another. But in JavaScript, instructions can be *asynchronous,* which means that you can't be confident that line five will always happen after line four. Imagine if you were getting dressed in the morning and it was possible to put your shoes on before your jeans (or your jeans on before your underpants)! That can happen in JavaScript.

A single-sentence metaphor and: *click!* the light comes on.

If the core of your talk is explaining a powerful new idea, it is helpful to ask: What do you assume your audience already knows? What will be your connecting theme? What are the concepts necessary to build your explanation? And what metaphors and examples will you use to reveal those concepts?

THE CURSE OF KNOWLEDGE

Unfortunately, this isn't that easy. We all suffer from a cognitive bias for which economist Robin Hogarth coined the term "the curse of knowledge." In a nutshell, we find it hard to remember what it feels like *not* to know something that we ourselves know well. A physicist lives and breathes subatomic particles and may assume that everyone else of course knows what a charm quark is. I was shocked in a recent cocktail-party discussion to hear a talented young novelist ask: "You keep using the term 'natural selection.' What exactly do you mean by that?" I thought everyone with half an education understood the basic ideas of evolution. I was wrong.

In *The Sense of Style: The Thinking Person's Guide to Writing in the 21st Century,* Steven Pinker suggests that overcoming the

curse of knowledge may be the single most important require-
ment in becoming a clear writer. If it's true about writing, when
readers have a chance to pause and reread a sentence several
times before continuing, then it's even more true about speaking. Pinker suggests that simply being conscious of this bias is not
enough. You have to expose your drafts to friends or colleagues
and beg for ruthless feedback on anything they don't understand.
The same is true for talks, and especially those talks that seek to
explain something complex. First share a draft script with colleagues and friends. Then try it out in front of a private audience.
And specifically ask the questions, *Did that make sense? Was anything confusing?*

I've long admired Pinker's ability to explain our minds' mach-
inations, so I asked him for some more guidance here. He told
me that, for true understanding to take place, the full *hierarchical
structure* of an idea must be communicated.

> A major finding of cognitive psychology is that long-term
> memory depends on coherent hierarchical organization of con-
> tent — chunks within chunks within chunks. A speaker's chal-
> lenge is to use the fundamentally one-dimensional medium of
> speech (one word after another) to convey a multidimensional
> (hierarchical and cross-linking) structure. A speaker begins
> with a web of ideas in his head, and by the very nature of lan-
> guage he has to convert it into a string of words.

This takes great care, right down to individual sentences and
how they link. A speaker has to be sure that listeners know how
each sentence relates logically to the preceding one, whether the
relationship is similarity, contrast, elaboration, exemplification,
generalization, before-and-after, cause, effect, or violated expectation. And they must know whether the point they are now pon-
dering is a digression, a part of the main argument, an exception
to the main argument, and so on.

If you imagine the structure of an explanatory talk as a central throughline with other parts connected to it — anecdotes, examples, amplifications, digressions, clarifications, etc. — then overall that structure may look like a tree. The throughline is the trunk, and the branches are the various pieces attached to it. But for understanding to take place, it's crucial the listener knows where she is on that tree.

This is often where the curse of knowledge strikes hardest. Every sentence is understandable, but the speaker forgets to show how they link together. To him, it's obvious.

Here's a simple example. A speaker says:

> Chimpanzees have vastly greater strength than humans. Humans learned how to use tools to amplify their natural strength. Of course, chimpanzees also use tools.

And an audience is left confused. What is the point being made here? Maybe the speaker was trying to argue that tools matter more than strength but didn't want to imply that chimpanzees never use tools. Or that chimpanzees are now capable of learning how to amplify their already greater strength. The three sentences don't connect, and the result is a muddle. The above should have been replaced with one of these:

> Although chimpanzees have vastly greater strength than humans, humans are much better tool users. And those tools have amplified human's natural strength far beyond that of chimpanzees'.

Or (and with a very different meaning),

> Chimpanzees have vastly greater strength than humans. And now we've discovered that they also use tools. They could use those tools to learn how to amplify their natural strength.

What this means is that some of the most important elements

in a talk are the little phrases that give clues to the talk's overall structure: "Although . . ." "One recent example . . ." "On the other hand . . ." "Let's build on that . . ." "Playing devil's advocate for a moment . . ." "I must just tell you two stories that amplify this finding." "As an aside . . ." "At this point you may object that . . ." "So, in summary . . ."

Equally important is the precise sequencing of sentences and concepts so that understanding can build naturally. In sharing early drafts of this book there were countless occasions when people pointed out, "I think I get it. But it would be much clearer if you switched these two paragraphs and explained the link between them a little better." It's important to achieve clarity in a book, and it's even more important to have clarity in a talk. Ultimately, your best bet is to recruit help from people new to the topic, because they will be best at spotting the gaps.

TED speaker Deborah Gordon, who explained how ant colonies can teach us crucial networking ideas, told me that the quest for explanation gaps was a crucial part of talk preparation:

> A talk isn't a container or a bin that you put content in, it's a process, a trajectory. The goal is to take the listener from where he is to someplace new. That means trying to make the sequence so stepwise that no one gets lost along the way. Not to be grandiose, but if you could fly and you wanted someone to fly with you, you would take their hand and take off and not let go, because once the person drops, that's it! I rehearsed in front of friends and acquaintances who knew nothing about the topic, asking them where they were puzzled or what they wondered about, hoping that by filling those gaps for them I'd be filling the same gaps for other people.

It's especially important to do a jargon check. Any technical terms or acronyms that may be unfamiliar to your listeners should be eliminated or explained. Nothing frustrates an audience more than to hear a 3-minute discussion of TLAs when they have no idea what TLAs are.* Maybe one such transgression can be handled, but when jargon terms pile up, people simply switch off.

I am *not* advocating that everything be explained on a level appropriate for sixth-graders. At TED we have a guideline based on Einstein's dictum, "Make everything as simple as it can be. But no simpler."† You don't want to insult your audience's intelligence. Sometimes specialist terms are essential. For most audiences, you don't have to spell out that DNA is a special molecule that carries unique genetic information. And you don't have to *over*-explain. Indeed, the best explainers say just enough to let people feel like they're coming up with the idea for themselves. Their strategy is to bring in the new concept and describe its shape just enough so that the prepared minds of the audience can snap it into place for themselves. That's time-efficient for you and deeply satisfying for them. By the end of the talk they're basking in the glow of their own smarts.

FROM EXPLANATION TO EXCITEMENT

There's one other key explanation tool. Before you try to build your idea, consider making clear what it *isn't*. You'll notice I've used that technique in this book already, for example, by discussing talk styles that don't work before going on to those that do. If an explanation is building a small mental model in a large space of possibilities, it's helpful first to reduce the size of that space. By ruling out plausible possibilities you make it a lot easier for your audience to close in on what it is you have in mind.

---

* TLA = Three Letter Acronym

† It's not clear he said it in exactly those words, but the idea is credited to him.

When, for instance, neuroscientist Sandra Aamodt wanted to explain why mindfulness was helpful for dieting, she said: "I'm not saying you need to learn to meditate or take up yoga. I'm talking about mindful *eating:* learning to understand your body's signals so that you eat when you're hungry and stop when you're full."

Superb TED Talk explainers include Hans Rosling (revelatory animated charts), David Deutsch (outside-the-box scientific thinking), Nancy Kanwisher (accessible neuroscience), Steven Johnson (where ideas come from), and David Christian (history on a grand canvas). I thoroughly recommend them all. They each build inside you something new and powerful that you will value forever.

If you can explain something well, you can use that ability to create real excitement in your audience. Bonnie Bassler is a scientist working on how bacteria communicate with each other. She gave a talk that dove into some pretty complex but mindblowing research her lab had been undertaking. By helping us understand it, she opened up a world of intriguing possibilities. Here's how.

She started by making the talk relevant to us. After all, it's not a given that anyone in the audience actually cared that much about bacteria. So she began like this:

I know you guys think of yourself as humans, and this is sort of how I think of you. There's about a trillion human cells that make each one of us who we are and able to do all the things that we do, but you have ten trillion bacterial cells in you or on you at any moment in your life. So, ten times more bacterial cells than human cells on a human being . . . These bacteria are not passive riders, they are incredibly important; they keep us alive. They cover us in an invisible body armor that keeps environmental insults out so that we stay healthy. They digest our food, they make our vitamins, they actually educate your immune system to keep bad microbes out. So they do all these amazing things that help us and are vital for keeping us alive, and they never get any press for that.

OK. Now it's personal. These bugs matter to us. Next, an unexpected question stirs our curiosity:

The question we had is how could they do anything at all? I mean, they're incredibly small; you have to have a microscope to see one. They live this sort of boring life where they grow and divide, and they've always been considered to be these asocial, reclusive organisms. And so it seemed to us that they are just too small to have an impact on the environment if they simply act as individuals.

This is getting intriguing. She's going to tell us that somehow bacteria hunt in packs? I'm eager to know more! Bonnie then takes us on a detective's investigation through various clues that point to how bacteria must act in concert. There's an amazing story about a bioluminescent squid that uses the synced-up behavior of bacteria to make itself invisible. And finally we get to her discovery of how invasive bacteria might launch an attack on a human. They can't do it individually. Instead, they emit a communication molecule. As more bacteria multiply in your body, the concentration of this molecule increases until suddenly they all "know" collectively that there are enough of them to attack, and they all begin emitting toxins at the same time. It's called *quorum sensing*. Wow!

She said this discovery opened up new strategies for fighting bacteria. Don't kill them, just cut their communication channels. With antibiotic immunity spreading, that is a truly exciting concept.

Then she ended her talk by teasing up an even broader implication:

> I would argue . . . that this is the invention of multicellularity. Bacteria have been on the earth for billions of years; humans, [a] couple hundred thousand. We think bacteria made the rules for how multicellular organization works . . . if we can figure them out in these primitive organisms, the hope is that they will be applied to other human diseases and human behaviors as well.

At every stage of Bonnie's talk, each piece was carefully built only on what came before. There was not a single piece of jargon that wasn't explained. And that gave her the ability to open new doors of possibility for us. It was complex science, but it got our nonexpert audience wildly excited, and at the end, much to her astonishment, we all stood and applauded her.

You can't give a powerful new idea to an audience unless you can learn how to explain. That can only be done step by step, fueled by curiosity. Each step builds on what the listener already knows. Metaphors and examples are essential to revealing how an idea is pieced together. Beware the curse of knowledge! You must be sure you're not making assumptions that will lose your audience. And when you've explained something special, excitement and inspiration will follow close behind.

8

PERSUASION

Reason Can Change Minds Forever

If explanation is building a brand-new idea inside someone's mind, persuasion is a little more radical. Before construction, it first requires some demolition.

Persuasion means convincing an audience that the way they currently see the world isn't quite right. And that means taking down the parts that aren't working, as well as rebuilding something better. When this works, it's thrilling for both speaker and audience.

Cognitive scientist Steven Pinker blew up my mental model of violence.

Anyone who grows up on a normal media diet assumes that our world is crippled by constant violence — wars, murders, assaults, terrorism — and that it seems to be getting worse. Pinker, in just 18 minutes, persuaded the TED audience that this assumption was dead wrong. That actually, when you pulled the camera back and looked at the real data, the world is becoming less violent, and that this trend has extended across years, decades, centuries, and millennia.

How did he do it? First with a little demolition. Our minds need to be primed before they can be persuaded. Pinker started by reminding people how hideous some of the violent practices of earlier eras had been, like the French public entertainment of five hundred years ago of lowering live cats into a fire to hear them shriek. Or the fact that, in many ancient societies, more than a third of adult males died in violence. Essentially he was saying, *You may think violence is getting worse, but you've forgotten just how awful it really was historically.*

Then he showed how modern media have an incentive to lead with stories of drama and violence, regardless of whether those events are representative of life as a whole. He was revealing a mechanism by which we might plausibly be overestimating the actual levels of violence out there.

With this priming in place, it was much easier to take seriously his statistics and charts, which showed substantial declines in all forms of violence, from murder to major wars. One key strategy here was to present the stats as relative to population size. What matters is not the total number of violent deaths but the chance that you individually will meet a violent death.

He went on to discuss four possible explanations for this unexpected trend and ended with this beautifully upbeat statement:

> Whatever its causes, the decline of violence, I think, has profound implications. It should force us to ask not just, why is there war? But also, why is there peace? Not just, what are we doing wrong? But also, what have we been doing right? Because we have been doing something right, and it sure would be good to find out what it is.

The talk led, four years later, to a major book, *The Better Angels of Our Nature*, which further developed his argument.

Let's assume that Pinker is right. If so, he has given a beautiful gift to millions of people. Most of us spend our whole lives under the assumption that the daily news is forever getting worse and that wars and terrorism and violence are out of control. When you replace that with the possibility that, even though things can be bad, they're actually on an upward trend, what a cloud that lifts! Persuasion can alter someone's outlook forever.

PERSUASION AND PRIMING

Psychologist Barry Schwartz changed the way I think about choice. In the West, we're obsessed with maximizing choice. Freedom is our mantra, and maximizing choice is the way to maximize freedom. Schwartz begs to differ. In his talk on the paradox of choice, he gradually builds the case that, in numerous circumstances, too much choice actually makes us *unhappy*. His demolition toolkit was surprisingly painless. He mixed snippets of psychological theory with a series of examples ranging from health insurance behavior to a frustrating shopping experience, all interspersed with delightful on-topic *New Yorker* cartoons. The ideas were counterintuitive, but the journey was thoroughly enjoyable, and we almost didn't notice that a worldview we all grew up with was being smashed to pieces.

Author Elizabeth Gilbert showed how the power of storytelling can be a key part of the persuasion toolkit. Her goal was to change the way we thought about creative genius. Instead of imagining that genius is part of some people's makeup and you either have it or you don't, think of it as something that you may *receive* from time to time as a gift, if you make yourself ready for it. Put just like that, it may not sound very convincing, but Gilbert used her brilliance as a storyteller to persuade us otherwise. She opened up with her own tale of terror at the prospect of having to repeat the success of her bestseller *Eat, Pray, Love* and shared hilarious and touching stories of famous creatives beset by angst over their inability to perform on demand. She also showed how the term *genius* was viewed differently in history, not as something you were, but as something that came to you. Only then could she share a story about the poet Ruth Stone, who told her of the moment when she sensed that a poem was coming.

And she felt it coming, because it would shake the earth under her feet. She knew that she had only one thing to do at that point, and that was to, in her words, run like hell. And she would run like hell to the house and she would be getting chased by this poem, and the whole deal was that she had to get to a piece of paper and a pencil fast enough so that when it thundered through her, she could collect it and grab it on the page.

What would have seemed an outlandish story if presented at the start of the talk seemed thoroughly natural by the end, and it cemented her core idea into place.

In each case, the key to prompting that worldview shift is to take the journey one step at a time, priming our minds in several different ways before getting to the main argument.

What do I mean by *priming?* The philosopher Daniel Dennett explains it best. He coined the term *intuition pump* to refer to any metaphor or linguistic device that intuitively makes a conclusion seem more plausible. This is priming. It is not a rigorous argument; it is simply a way of nudging someone in your direction. Barry Schwartz's shopping story was an intuition pump. Had he just gone straight to "Too many choices can make you unhappy," we might have been skeptical. Instead he primed us:

There was a time when jeans came in one flavor, and you bought them, and they fit like crap, they were really uncomfortable, but if you wore them and washed them enough times, they started to feel OK. I went to replace my jeans after years of wearing these old ones, and I said, "I want a pair of jeans. Here's my size." And the shopkeeper said, "Do you want slim fit, easy fit, relaxed fit? You want button fly or zipper fly? You want stonewashed or acid-washed? Do you want them distressed? You want boot cut, tapered, blah blah blah."

As he tells the story, we sense his stress and we remember all the times we have ourselves been stressed by endless shopping excursions. Even though his story is a single story of a single man and can't possibly by itself justify the statement that too much choice makes you unhappy, nonetheless we get where he is heading. Suddenly, the case he's building seems a lot more plausible.

Dennett points out that many of the most revered passages of philosophical writing are not reasoned arguments, but powerful intuition pumps like Plato's cave or Descartes' demon. In the latter, Descartes wanted to doubt everything that could be doubted, so he imagined his entire conscious experience as a deception foisted on him by a malicious demon. The demon could have invented the entire world he thought he saw. The only thing Descartes could be certain of was the experience of thinking and doubting, but that at least meant he existed. Hence: I think, therefore I am. Without the demon, the logic is hard to fathom. Our minds are not robotic logic machines. They need to be nudged in the right direction, and intuition pumps are vivid ways to do this.

Once people have been primed, it's much easier to make your main argument. And how do you do *that?* By using the most noble tool of them all, a tool that can wield the most impact over the very long term. And it's named using an old-fashioned philosophical word that I love: *Reason.*

THE LONG REACH OF REASON

The thing about reason is that it's capable of delivering a conclusion at a whole different level of certainty than any other mental tool. In a reasoned argument, provided the starting assumptions are true, then the validly reasoned conclusions must also be true and can be *known* to be true. If you can walk someone through a reasoned argument convincingly, the idea you have planted in her mind will lodge there and never let go.

But for the process to work, it must be broken down into small steps, each of which must be totally convincing. The starting point of each step is something the audience can clearly see to be true, or it's something that was shown to be true earlier in the talk. So the core mechanism here is if-then: if X is true, dear friends, then, clearly, Y follows (because *every* X implies a Y).

One of the TED Talks rated most persuasive is that of charity reformer Dan Pallotta, who argues that the way we think about charity means that our nonprofit organizations are hopelessly handicapped. To make his case, he takes five different aspects of an organization: salary levels, marketing expectations, willingness to take risks, time allowed for impact, and access to capital. In each case he uses razor-sharp language backed by beautiful infographics to show an absurd dichotomy between what we expect of our companies and our nonprofits. And the talk is simply teeming with compelling if-then statements.

For example, after pointing out that we encourage companies to take risks but frown on nonprofits for doing so, he has this statement. "Well, you and I know when you prohibit failure, you kill innovation. If you kill innovation in fundraising, you can't raise more revenue. If you can't raise more revenue, you can't grow. And if you can't grow, you can't possibly solve large social problems." QED. Case proven. If we want our nonprofits to solve large social problems, we must *not* prohibit them from failure.

There's another form of reasoned argument, known as *reductio ad absurdum*, that can be devastatingly powerful. It is the process of taking the *counter* position to what you're arguing and showing that it leads to a contradiction. If that counter position is false, your position is strengthened (or even proven, if there are no other possible positions that could be taken). Speakers rarely engage in the full, rigorous version of reductio ad absurdum. But they often tap into its spirit by offering a dramatic counterexample and showing it to be self-evidently ridiculous. Here's another snippet from Dan Pallotta's talk. He's arguing that it's crazy how we frown on high salaries for nonprofit leaders. "You want to make fifty million dollars selling violent video games to kids, go for it. We'll put you on the cover of *Wired* magazine. But you want to make half a million dollars trying to cure kids of malaria, you're considered a parasite yourself." Rhetorically, that's a home run.

Undercutting the credibility of the opposite position is another powerful device, but it needs to be handled with care. It's better used on issues than directly on opponents. I'm fine with: "It's not hard to understand why we've been given a different impression by the media on this for years. You sell newspapers with drama, not boring scientific evidence." But uncomfortable with: "Of course he says that. He's paid to say that." That can drift very quickly from reason to mudslinging.

MAKE US DETECTIVES

Here's a more attractive way to build a case. At TED, we call it the *detective story*. Some of the most compelling persuasion talks are structured entirely around this device. You start with the big mystery, then travel the world of ideas in search of possible solutions to it, ruling them out one by one, until there's only one viable solution that survives.

A simple example is artist Siegfried Woldhek's talk. He wanted to prove that three famous Leonardo da Vinci drawings were actually self-portraits from different stages of his life. To make the case, he framed the talk as his quest to discover "the true face" of Leonardo da Vinci. He starts with a full palette of the 120 portraits of males that Leonardo is credited with, and asks: Were any of these self-portraits? How could we know? And then, like a detective eliminating suspects, he starts cutting them down, using his own skills as a portrait painter, until only three remain.

Next, the clincher. Although they depict men of different ages, and they were painted at different times, they all share the same facial features. And they match a statue of da Vinci, the only proven third-party image of him.

What makes this persuasive is that we feel as if we have gone on the same learning journey as the speaker. Instead of being told facts, we've been invited to join the process of discovery. Our minds are naturally more engaged. As we eliminate rival theories one by one, we gradually become convinced. *We persuade ourselves.*

This device can be used to turn the most daunting topic into something truly intriguing. A regular challenge for speakers is how to turn difficult subjects like disease or starvation or human degradation into talks that audiences will show up for and engage with.

Economist Emily Oster wanted to persuade us that the tools of economics could allow us to think differently about HIV/AIDS, but instead of just presenting an economic argument, she became a detective. She presented a slide titled FOUR THINGS WE KNOW. Taking each one in turn, she presented some surprising pieces of evidence and effectively demolished them, one by one, opening the door for her to present an alternative theory.

The power of this structure is that it taps deep into our love of stories. The whole talk feels like a story — better yet, a mystery story. Curiosity builds to more curiosity through to a satisfying conclusion. But at the same time, there's a powerful logic underlying it. If each of these alternatives is false, and there's only one other viable alternative, then that alternative must be true. Case solved!

IT WILL TAKE MORE THAN LOGIC

It can sometimes be hard to make reason-based talks really come alive. People aren't computers, and their logic circuits aren't always the ones they engage most easily. To make a talk truly persuasive, it is not enough to build it out of watertight logical steps. Those are necessary, to be sure, but not sufficient. Most people are capable of being convinced by logic, but they aren't always energized by it. And without being energized, they may quickly forget the argument and move on. So the language of reason may have to be bolstered by other tools that make the conclusions not just valid, but meaningful, exciting, desirable.

There are lots of tools you can use here, in addition to the intuition pumps mentioned earlier, or the detective story approach.

- **Inject some humor early on.** This communicates a useful message: *I'm going to pull you through some demanding thinking . . . but it's going to be fun. We'll sweat together and laugh together.*
- **Add an anecdote.** Maybe one that reveals how you got engaged in this issue. It humanizes you. If people know *why* you're passionate about the issue, they're more likely to listen to your logic.
- **Offer vivid examples.** If I wanted to persuade you that external reality is nothing like you believe it to be, I might first show a slide of a dramatic optical illusion. Just because something *looks* a certain way, doesn't make it so.
- **Recruit third-party validation.** *"My colleagues at Harvard and I have spent ten years looking at the data, and we've unanimously concluded it has to be seen this way."* Or, *"And that's why it's not just me arguing this; every mother of a two-year-old boy knows this to be true."* Statements like these

need careful handling as neither is a valid argument in itself, but, depending on the audience, they may make your argument more persuasive.

- **Use powerful visuals.** At one point in his talk, Dan Pallotta uses pie charts to show the results of two nonprofits' fundraising efforts. First, a bake sale with 5 percent overhead, and second, a professional fundraising enterprise with 40 percent overhead. The second one looks terrible, wasteful, until Dan says:

> We confuse morality with frugality. We've all been taught that the bake sale with 5 percent overhead is morally superior to the professional fundraising enterprise with 40 percent overhead, but we're missing the most important piece of information, which is: What is the actual size of these pies? What if the bake sale only netted seventy-one dollars for charity because it made no investment in its scale, and the professional fundraising enterprise netted 71 million dollars because it did? Now which pie would we prefer, and which pie do we think people who are hungry would prefer?

While he's speaking, the second pie chart expands and the first one shrinks. The non-overhead portion of the second chart is now vastly bigger than that in the first. His point lands with great impact.

Dan Pallotta's talk won a huge standing ovation and has been seen more than 3 million times. Three months after it was posted, the three biggest charity evaluation agencies put out a joint press release that took on board many of his arguments, concluding that, "The people and communities served by charities don't need low overhead, they need high performance."

But not every talk that is reason based will see such immediate success. These talks are generally harder to process than some others, and they may not be the most popular. However, I believe they are among the most important talks on our site, because *reason is the best way of building wisdom for the long term.* A robust argument, even if it isn't immediately accepted by everyone, will gradually gather new adherents until it becomes unstoppable.

Indeed, there's a TED Talk specifically about this: a Socratic dialogue between psychologist Steven Pinker and philosopher Rebecca Newberger Goldstein in which she gradually persuades him that reason is the deepest underlying force behind moral progress throughout history. Not empathy, not cultural evolution, although those have played their parts. Reason. Sometimes its influence can take centuries to be realized. In the talk, Goldstein shares powerful quotes from history's reasoners on slavery, gender inequality, and gay rights that predate the movements they inspired by more than a hundred years. Nonetheless, these arguments were key to the success of those movements.

The Pinker/Goldstein dialogue may be the single most important argument contained in any TED Talk, yet, as of 2015 it has fewer than 1 million views. Reason is not a fast-growing weed, but a slow-growing oak tree. Nonetheless, its roots run deep and strong, and once grown it can transform a landscape forever. I am hungry for many more reason-based talks on TED.

In three sentences . . .

- Persuasion is the act of replacing someone's worldview with something better.
- And at its heart is the power of reason, capable of long-term impact.
- Reason is best accompanied by intuition pumps, detective stories, visuals, or other plausibility-priming devices.

9
REVELATION
Take My Breath Away!

Connection, narration, explanation, persuasion . . . all vital tools. But what's the most direct way of gifting an idea to an audience?

Simply *show* it to them.

Many talks are anchored this way. You reveal your work to the audience in a way that delights and inspires.

The generic name for this is *revelation.* In a talk based on revelation, you might:

- Show a series of images from a brand-new art project and talk through it
- Give a demo of a product you've invented
- Describe your vision for a self-sustaining city of the future
- Show fifty stunning photos from your recent trip through the Amazon jungle

There's an infinite variety of possible revelation talks, and their success depends on what is being revealed.

In a talk based on images, your main goal might just be to create a sense of wonder and aesthetic delight. If it's a demo, you're probably seeking to amaze and to create a new sense of possibility. If it's a vision of the future, you want it to be so vivid and compelling that your audience makes it their own.

Let's take these three broad categories and dig in deeper.

THE WONDER WALK

A wonder walk is a talk based on the revelation of a succession of images or wonder moments. If a talk is a journey, then a wonder walk can be thought of as a studio tour with an artist who gives you revealing insights into each artwork. Or a hike in dramatic terrain with a great explorer as your guide. Each step is a simple one, from one piece of work to the next, with a sense of wonder building all the while. *"If you liked that . . . just wait till you see this!"*

Assuming the work is strong, the journey can be enjoyable, informative, or inspiring. This talk structure is most often used by artists, designers, photographers, and architects, although anyone with a body of visual work can use it. Including scientists.

For example, David Gallo's brief talk on underwater astonishments was a glorious wonder walk — or, in this case, a wonder dive. He showed us a series of incredible images and videos of bioluminescent creatures that a science-fiction artist could barely imagine. This was followed by astonishing footage of an octopus vanishing from view by changing its skin pattern in an instant to exactly match that of the coral behind it. And Gallo's excitement at the awesomeness of exotic ocean life quickly became infectious. As well as describing what we were seeing, he provided context that had the effect of dialing up the sense of wonder.

That's the unknown world, and today we've only explored about 3 percent of what's out there in the ocean. Already we've found the world's highest mountains, the world's deepest valleys, underwater lakes, underwater waterfalls . . . And in a place where we thought [there was] no life at all, we find more life . . . and diversity and density than the tropical rainforest, which tells us that we don't know much about this planet at all. There's still 97 percent, and either that 97 percent is empty or just full of surprises.

It's just a 5-minute talk with a simple structure. But it's been seen more than 12 million times.

Another simple but super-compelling wonder walk was science writer Mary Roach's talk on orgasm. She walked us through ten things we never knew about orgasm, including a video of a Dutch farmer with a pig that you perhaps should not watch in the company of either your parents or your children! Wonder walks don't have to be earnest. They can be funny, provocative, and punchy.

The appeal of this type of talk from a speaker's point of view is that the structure is clear. You're simply walking the audience through your work, or through something you're passionate about, one piece at a time. Each piece is accompanied by slides or video, and you simply proceed from one to the next, building excitement as you go.

But wonder walks work best when there's a clear linking theme. Something stronger than just a series of recent examples of your work. Without that, this type of talk can quickly become tedious. "Now we'll turn to my next project" is a flat transition line that invites the audience to start shifting in their seats. Much stronger is to give us a link. "This next project took that idea and dialed it up by an order of magnitude . . ."

And stronger still is to have a throughline that pulls all the pieces together. Shea Hembrey took us through "an exhibition of a hundred artists' work." Each piece was completely different . . . paintings, sculptures, photographs, videos, and mixed media, covering a vast swath of artistic ideas. The throughline? Every artist was him! Yup, Shea had created every single work. Because of that, the more wildly different each new piece was, the more our sense of wonder grew.

There are many ways the wonder walk can go wrong, however. Foremost is when the work is described in inaccessible language. Some professions have a ghastly tradition of using needlessly obscure, overintellectualized language to describe their work, with art and architecture topping the list. When practitioners feel the need to use that same language in a talk, they shouldn't be surprised to see their invited guests quietly slipping out the back door. *In this work I sought to challenge the paradigm of identity versus communality in the context of a postmodernist dialectic . . .* If you're ever tempted to say anything remotely like that, please, please take out your sharpest pair of scissors and slash it out of your script.

Steven Pinker pointed out to me that this type of language is much worse than simply the misuse of jargon.

> *Paradigm* and *dialectic* are not technical terms like DNA that specialists can't avoid. They're metaconcepts — concepts about other concepts, rather than concepts about things in the world. Academese, bizspeak, corporate boilerplate, and art-critic bafflegab are tedious and incomprehensible because they are filled with metaconcepts like approach, assumption, concept, condition, context, framework, issue, level, model, perspective, process, range, role, strategy, tendency, and variable.

There's a valid use for these terms individually. But use them sparingly. When they pile up on each other, you're endangering audience comprehension.

Instead, the goal should be to give us the inside scoop. Share with us, *in accessible human language,* what you were dreaming of when you started the work. Show us your creative process. How did you get there? What mistakes did you make along the way? When illustrator David Macaulay shared his drawings of Rome, he showed not just the finished works, but his mistakes and dead ends and how he got from there to the published illustrations. That meant that every creative person in the room could learn something from it. Lifting the lid on your process is one of the key gifts of any creative talk.

Above all, design the talk to give us maximum experience of the work itself. If your work is visual, consider cutting way back the number of words you use, and instead put the focus on the visuals. A 12-minute talk can comfortably reveal more than 100 images. Perhaps some sequences are allowed just 2 seconds of screen time per slide. And they can be amplified in their power by a tool all too rarely used by speakers: *silence.* One of the best examples on TED of a wonder walk is by kinetic sculptor Reuben Margolin. His voice is the whispered backdrop to his astonishing works, the perfect spoken captions to a gallery of pure inspiration. And he has the courage to be silent from time to time. Some of the most powerful moments of the talk come when, having set the context, he lets us simply immerse visually in his work.

One clever way to ensure that the walk maintains energy is to make the slides automatically advance. Take a look at Ross Lovegrove's engaging walk through his nature-inspired design projects for a superb example of this. More than one hundred slides and videos of his work are revealed in a pre-timed sequence, and Lovegrove simply talks about each as it arrives, the format ensuring a dynamic pace. Louis Schwartzberg did something similar with his talk about his astonishing movie *Mysteries of the Unseen World.* He let clips of the movie play through the whole talk, while his voice acts as lyrical narration. The result is jaw-dropping impact.

Many talks given within companies could be improved if they were thought of as wonder walks. Presentations that plod through your department's recent work bullet point by bullet point can quickly get boring. Suppose, instead, an effort were made to ask: How can we link these projects together to build excitement? How can we communicate what is delightful, unexpected, or humorous about them? How can we switch the tone from "look what we've achieved" to "look how intriguing this is"? Suppose, instead of a series of bullet points, there was an attempt to pair each step of the walk with an intriguing image? Suppose there was a real effort to figure out what unique and shareable idea you've uncovered that others in the company could benefit from? Ah, now that could be a talk worth shutting down your iPhone for.

Whether it's business, science, design, or art, don't just walk people through your work. Figure out the route that engages, intrigues, and enlightens. The route that brings in a little wonder and delight.

THE DYNAMIC DEMO

Suppose what you're revealing is not just visual, it's a technology, an invention, or a brand-new process. Then it's not enough just to look at it. We need to see it working. We need a demonstration.

Great demos can be the most memorable part of any conference. Right there, live on stage, you snatch a little glimpse of the future.

When Jeff Han showed the potential for multi-touch technology back in 2006, two years before the iPhone was launched, you could hear the audience gasp. Pranav Mistry's demo of Sixth-Sense technology had similar impact, revealing the amazing possibilities when you combined a cell phone with a personal projector and a camera that can detect your gestures. For example, just framing a distant object with your fingers would take a photo of it that could then be displayed on any nearby white surface.

To give such a talk, the single thing that matters most, of course, is the quality of whatever it is you're going to demonstrate. Is it truly a compelling invention or design? Assuming it is, there are numerous ways to unveil it. What you shouldn't do is spend the first half of the talk giving a complicated context to the technology. Your audience hasn't yet seen it in action and may switch off.

When you have something amazing to show, allow yourself to indulge in a little showmanship. I don't mean that you should start sounding glib and puffed up, but you should excite us a little. Give us a hint of what we're about to see. *Then* take us through the necessary context, ideally building toward a powerful climax, once the groundwork has been laid.

Markus Fischer is an incredible inventor. At TEDGlobal in Edinburgh in 2011 he showed off an extraordinary robot that looked — and flew — like a giant seagull. In fact, it was so realistic that, when he flew it for us at the picnic after the event, it was poop-attacked by a flock of real seagulls, clearly startled by their new competitor. In his talk, he spent the first 10 minutes on the technicalities of flight, without really giving a hint at what was to come. He lost some of the audience. The jaw-dropping nature of the demo itself — flying his seagull around the auditorium — soon fixed that. But for the online version we changed the order of his talk a little so that he opened with the phrase "It is a dream of mankind to fly like a bird." That immediately gave beautiful context to the talk, helping it soar to millions of online views.

Jeff Han got it right, starting his talk like this:

I'm really excited to be here today. I'll show you some stuff that's just ready to come out of the lab, literally, and I'm glad that you guys are going to be among the first to see it in person, because I think this is going to really change the way we interact with machines from this point on.

In just a few words he had given intriguing hints that we were to get an exciting peek into the future. Now he was free to go ahead and explain the technology before showing it in action. He gave the background, then he started showing what the technology was capable of, drawing gasps and applause, and building amazement all the way.

Inventor Michael Pritchard used a similar structure. First he shared a quick thought experiment on how life would be without safe drinking water. Then he embarked on an explanation of the technology behind the "lifesaver bottle" he'd designed. Some might have ended the talk there. But the power of the talk was in showing, not telling, and Michael pulled out all the stops. He had a big glass container on stage, into which he poured muddy pond water, sewage runoff, and rabbit droppings, turning the water a nasty brown. Then he pumped it through his bottle into an empty glass and offered it to me to drink. Happily, it tasted just fine. And technological theory was turned into theatrical proof. Michael then went on to speak of the implications of his technology for disaster relief and for global public health; truth was, he'd already won over the audience with the powerful demo of the idea at work.

The structure Han and Pritchard used is good for most demos:

- An initial tease
- Necessary background, context, and/or the invention story
- The demo itself (the more visual and dramatic the better, so long as you're not faking it)
- The implications of the technology

Sometimes a demo is stunning enough that it allows an audience to imagine truly exciting applications and implications. And then the demo becomes not just a demo, but a vision of the future. That's where we turn next.

THE DREAMSCAPE

Humans have a skill that, so far as we know, no other species possesses. It is so important a skill that we have multiple words to label its different flavors: imagination, invention, innovation, design, vision. It is the ability to pattern the world in our minds and then re-pattern it to create a world that doesn't actually exist but someday might.

Amazingly, we are also able to reveal these nonexistent worlds to others, in the hope that they too may become excited by them. And occasionally, and even more miraculously, after several people share a vision among themselves, they are able to use it as a blueprint to actually make that world become real. The screenwriter persuades the studio to make the movie. The inventor persuades a company to build the gizmo. The architect persuades the client to fund the building. The entrepreneur energizes a startup team with the belief that they will reshape the future.

Dreams can be shared with images, with sketches, with demos . . . or just with words.

Some of the most powerful speeches in history have been powerful precisely because they communicated a dream with irresistible eloquence and passion. Most famously, of course, was Martin Luther King Jr. at the Lincoln Memorial in Washington, DC, on August 28, 1963. After carefully preparing the ground, and filling his audience with an intense desire to end centuries of injustice, he launched into it:

> I have a dream that one day this nation will rise up, live out the true meaning of its creed: "We hold these truths to be self-evident, that all men are created equal."
>
> I have a dream that one day on the red hills of Georgia sons

of former slaves and the sons of former slave-owners will be able to sit down together at the table of brotherhood . . .

I have a dream that my four little children will one day live in a nation where they will not be judged by the color of their skin but by the content of their character.

His speech lasted 17 minutes and 40 seconds. And it changed history.

President Kennedy took humankind to the moon by first sharing a dream. And some of the language he chose is surprising:

We choose to go to the moon in this decade and do the other things, not because they are easy, but because they are hard. . . . I realize that this is in some measure an act of faith and vision, for we do not now know what benefits await us. But if I were to say, my fellow citizens, that we shall send to the moon, 240,000 miles away from the control station in Houston, a giant rocket more than 300 feet tall, the length of this football field, made of new metal alloys, some of which have not yet been invented, capable of standing heat and stresses several times more than have ever been experienced, fitted together with a precision better than the finest watch, carrying all the equipment needed for propulsion, guidance, control, communications, food and survival, on an untried mission, to an unknown celestial body, and then return it safely to earth, re-entering the atmosphere at speeds of over 25,000 miles per hour, causing heat about half that of the temperature of the sun — almost as hot as it is here today — and do all this, and do it right, and do it first before this decade is out — then we must be bold . . . But it will be done. And it will be done before the end of this decade.

You might think that this framing of the initiative, as one fraught with peril and uncertainty, would be counterproductive. The reason it works is not just that it makes vivid what is to come.

It is that he is making us dream of heroism. He is giving us a trip into the future to read the narrative that will eventually be told about this endeavor.

At TED, most of our talks are told in more conversational language. But the ability to paint a compelling picture of the future is truly one of the greatest gifts a speaker can bring. Indeed, dreamscape speakers have been among TED's most thrilling. They speak not of the world as it is, but as it might be. When these talks are done right, they get an audience's hearts to pound and their minds to explode with a sense of possibility.

Salman Khan's vision for an education revolution in which video lessons allow kids to master topics at their own pace was revealed beautifully, piece by piece, and you could feel the excitement in the room building.

Filmmaker Chris Milk showed his work using virtual reality to powerfully re-create the experience of life inside a Syrian refugee camp. People worry that virtual reality will shut us off from each other. Milk offered a thrilling counterview; that virtual reality devices could become the ultimate empathy-generating machines.

Marine biologist Sylvia Earle used powerful images and eloquent language to describe the crisis presented by our overfished, overpolluted oceans. But she didn't stop there. She spoke of what might be if we began creating "hope spots," marine protected areas where sea life could recover. Her vision was so compelling that one audience member wrote her a check for $1 million on the spot and is still supporting her work six years later. In that time, the amount of protected space in our oceans worldwide has more than tripled.

There are two keys to sharing a dream effectively:

- Paint a bold picture of the alternative future you desire;
- Do so in such a way that others will also desire that future.

Doing both of these in the same talk is challenging. The first part often requires visual aids. Kent Larson spent 18 minutes sharing radical design ideas like folding cars and form-shifting apartments to allow more people to fit into cities without overcrowding. The individual ideas didn't necessarily look like surefire bets, but by revealing them visually, he made them seem much more convincing.

Architect Thomas Heatherwick included a slide in his talk that might be the single most appealing slide I've ever seen at TED. It showed a design for an apartment complex in Kuala Lumpur with elegant curved high-rise buildings that swelled out from a narrow base to allow space for a gorgeous park at ground level. It painted a picture of a future I would have been thrilled to have been born into.

But that's not always the case. Often, when technologies are unveiled, the audience doesn't know whether to be excited or to freak out. In 2012, the then head of DARPA, Regina Dugan, revealed a sequence of technologies, such as high-speed gliders and hummingbird drones, that were both jaw-dropping and somewhat disturbing, given their likely military use. And talks about genetic engineering, or a computer's ability to recognize faces in a crowd, or the development of humanlike robots, can seem more creepy than appealing.

How does a speaker avoid that kind of audience discomfort? The only way is to make it clear why this future is worth pursuing. Or present the idea in a way that emphasizes human values, not just clever technology.

Bran Ferren attempted this at TED2014. He spoke of how autonomous vehicles would usher in a dramatically different future. But his talk began with the inspiration he'd had as a child on a visit to the Pantheon in Rome with his parents, and it ended with a call to inspire the children of the future. "We need to encourage them to find their own path, even if it's very different from our own. We also need them to understand something that doesn't seem adequately appreciated in our increasingly tech-dependent world, that art and design are not luxuries, nor somehow incompatible with science and engineering. They are in fact essential to what makes us special." What could have been pure tech vision, and perhaps a little scary, ended up human and hopeful.

Humor helps too. Juan Enriquez has presented a series of mind-bending talks at TED, showcasing coming developments in biology and genetics that might have seemed deeply alarming if he didn't find a way of injecting a little laughter with every slide. With Juan at your side, the future seems wondrous rather than worrisome.

Finally, the more actionable a future vision can be, the better. StoryCorps founder Dave Isay spoke of the power of people asking those close to them deep questions about the meaning of their lives and recording those interviews. He then shared an app that would allow anyone to do this simply and to upload the result to the Library of Congress, creating a permanent record. His vision of a world in which people truly listened to each other was inspiring, and within days of his talk being released, thousands of people recorded meaningful conversations they'd never had before.

That's the power of our dreams. They can spread to others, build excitement and belief, and thereby make themselves come true. By giving us a sense of increased possibility, they also inspire us to work harder on our own dreams. If you're invited to go on a journey with an inspired dreamer, that's an invitation you can never refuse.

MIX AND MATCH

Here's the reality. Most talks do not fit neatly into just one of the categories we've discussed so far. Rather, they include elements from many of them. For example, Amy Cuddy's popular talk on how your body language affects your own confidence is an artful mix of explanation and personal storytelling. And Salman Khan's talk begins with his own story and morphs into a wonder walk through the remarkable features his Khan Academy is building, before ending up in dreamscape territory — a thrilling vision of the potential for a new type of education.

So I will reemphasize: *The above techniques are not to be seen as in any way limiting you.* They are tools to help you imagine how you can best undertake your own remarkable construction project in your listeners' minds. Select, mix, match, and augment in the way that works most powerfully and authentically for the idea you wish to build.

So, now let's assume you have the throughline, the talk content, and have woven together your own artful mix of connection, narration, explanation, persuasion, and revelation. What next?

It's time to get this show on the road.

We're going to look at four key elements of the talk-preparation process that will determine if your talk sings or croaks:

- Whether or not to include visuals, and if so, what visuals?
- Whether to script and memorize your talk, or plan to speak "in the moment"
- How to practice both types of talks
- And how to open and close for maximum impact

Are you ready? Come along; there's work to be done.

Preparation Process

10
VISUALS
Those Slides Hurt!

In the twenty-first century we have the ability to supplement the spoken word with a dazzling array of technologies that, done right, may take a talk to a whole new level. Photographs, illustrations, elegant typography, graphs, infographics, animation, video, audio, big data simulations — all can dial up both the explanatory power of a talk and its aesthetic appeal.

Despite this, the first question to ask yourself is whether you actually need any of it. It's a striking fact that at least a third of TED's most viewed talks make no use of slides whatsoever.

How can that be? Surely a talk plus images is always going to be more interesting than just a talk? Well no, actually. Slides move at least a little bit of attention away from the speaker and onto the screen. If the whole power of a talk is in the personal connection between speaker and audience, slides may actually get in the way of that.

Now, it is certainly not the case that there is a zero-sum attention tradeoff between screen and speaker. What is being shown onscreen often occupies a different mental category than what is being said. Aesthetic versus analytical, for example. Nonetheless, if the core of your talk is intensely personal, or if you have other devices for livening up your talk — like humor or vivid stories — then you may do better to forget the visuals and just focus on speaking personally to the audience.

And for every speaker, the following is true: Having no slides at all is better than bad slides.

Having said that, the majority of talks do benefit from great slides, and for some talks, the visuals are the absolute difference between success and failure.

TED was originally a conference devoted purely to technology, entertainment, and design, and the presence of designers quickly fostered the expectation that slides would be elegant and impactful. Arguably, that tradition is a core reason why TED Talks took off.

So what are the key elements to strong visuals?

They fall into three categories:

- Revelation
- Explanatory power
- Aesthetic appeal

Let's handle those in turn.

REVEAL!

The most obvious case for visuals is simply to show something that's hard to describe. Presenting the work of most artists and photographers of course depends on doing this. An explorer revealing a voyage or a scientist unveiling a discovery can also use visuals in this way.

Edith Widder was part of the team that first captured the giant squid on video. When she came to TED, her entire talk was built around that moment of revelation. When the incredible creature eventually appeared onscreen, the audience nearly jumped out of its skin. But use of images for revelation doesn't have to be as dramatic. The key is to set the context, prime the audience, and then

. . . BAM! Let the visuals work their magic. Run them full-screen, with minimal adornment.

EXPLAIN!

A picture is worth a thousand words (even though it takes words to express that concept). Often the best explanations happen when words and images work together. Your mind is an integrated system. Much of our world is imagined visually. If you want to really explain something new, often the simplest, most powerful way is to show and tell.

But for that to work, there needs to be a compelling fit between what you tell and what you show. Sometimes a speaker will hit the audience with a slide of immense complexity. Perhaps he is unconsciously trying to impress with the sheer scope and nuance of his work. As he continues churning out the words, the audience is desperately scanning the slide, trying to figure out how to match what is being said with what they are looking at.

The key to avoiding this is to limit each slide to a single core idea. Some speakers, and especially scientists, seem to have the unconscious operating assumption that they should minimize the number of slides, therefore cramming a ton of data onto each one. This may have been true in days when slides were physical things that you had to load into a slide projector. Today, though, the cost of ten slides is the same as the cost of one. The only thing that's limited is the time you have to deliver your talk. So an overly complex slide that might take 2 minutes to explain could be replaced with three or four simpler slides that you can click through in the same amount of time.

TED's Tom Rielly speaks about the need to manage cognitive load:

With a talk and slides you have two streams of cognitive output running in parallel. The speaker needs to blend both streams into a master mix. Talking about theoretical physics has a high cognitive load. So does a slide with dozens of elements. In these circumstances, the audience member's brain has to decide whether to focus on your words, your slides, or both, and it's mostly involuntary. So you must design where attention is going and make sure a high cognitive load on a slide doesn't fight with what you're saying.

Similarly, it doesn't make sense to leave a slide onscreen once you've finished talking about it. Here's Tom again.

Just go to a blank, black slide and then the audience will get a vacation from images and pay more attention to your words. Then, when you go back to slides, they will be ready to go back to work.

If your goal is one key idea per slide, then it makes sense to consider whether anything more can be done with a slide to highlight the point it is trying to make. This is especially true with graphs and charts. If you're talking about how rainfall in February is always greater than in October, and you show a graph of annual rainfall, why not give the audience the gift of highlighting February and October in different colors?

And if you then go on to make a comparison between March and November, do that with a separate build or on a separate slide with those months differentiated. Don't leave it all crammed on one slide.

David McCandless is a master at turning data into understanding by the use of elegant slides. At TEDGlobal in 2010, for example, he showed two slides. The first was titled WHO HAS THE BIGGEST MILITARY BUDGET? It showed ten squares of different sizes, each square representing a country, in proportion to the size of their budgets. The US, of course, was the largest by far.

The second slide, however, showed squares representing military budget as a percentage of GDP. And suddenly the US is in eighth place, behind Myanmar, Jordan, Georgia, and Saudi Arabia. In just two slides, your worldview is sharpened dramatically.

Other speakers still seem to believe that you enhance the explanatory power of your slides by filling them with words, often the same words that they plan to utter. Nothing could be farther from the truth. Those classic PowerPoint slide decks with a headline followed by multiple bullet points of long phrases are the surest single way to lose an audience's attention altogether. The reason is that the audience reads ahead of the speaker, and by the time the speaker covers a specific point, it feels old hat. When we see speakers come to TED with slide decks like this, we pour them a drink, go and sit with them at a computer monitor, and gently ask their permission to delete, delete, delete. Maybe each bullet point becomes its own slide; many phrases are reduced to a single phrase; they're replaced by an image; or they are deleted altogether.

The point is there is no value in simply repeating in text what you are saying on stage. Conceivably, if you are developing a point over a couple of minutes, it may be worth having a word or a phrase onscreen to remind people of the topic at hand. But otherwise, words on the screen are fighting your presentation, not enhancing it.

Even when a text slide is simple, it may be indirectly stealing your thunder. Instead of a slide that reads: *A black hole is an object so massive that no light can escape from it,* you'd do better with one that reads: *How black is a black hole?* Then you'd give the information from that original slide in spoken form. That way, the slide teases the audience's curiosity and makes your words *more* interesting, not less.

When you think about it, it's fairly simple. The main purpose of visuals can't be to communicate words; your mouth is perfectly good at doing that. It's to share things your mouth can't do so well: photographs, video, animations, key data.

Used this way, the screen can explain in an instant what might take hours otherwise. At TED, our favorite proponent of explanatory visuals is Hans Rosling. Back in 2006, he unveiled an animated graphic sequence that lasted just 48 seconds. But in those 48 seconds he transformed everyone's mental model of the developing world. And here's the thing: If you haven't seen it, I can't actually explain it to you. To try would take several paragraphs, and even then I wouldn't be close. That's the whole point. It *had* to be shown on a screen. So next time you're near a computer, Google "Hans Rosling: The best stats you've ever seen." Watch and marvel. (The 48-second clip starts at 4:05.)

Not everyone can be a Hans Rosling. But everyone can at least ask themselves the question, *Are visuals key to explaining what I want to say? And, if so, how do I best combine them with my words so that they're working powerfully together?*

DELIGHT!

An often overlooked contribution of visuals is their ability to give a talk immense aesthetic appeal.

It amazes me that visual artists will often restrict what they show to just a tiny fraction of their work. Yes, *concepts* in a talk need to be limited. But images? Not so much. The mistake is to assume that you have to *explain* every image. You don't. If you had invited a prized audience into your own vast exhibition hall to see your work, but you only had time to focus on a single gallery, you would nonetheless first lead them quickly through the rest of the hall, if only to take their breath away and expand their understanding of your broader body of work. With images, a 5-second viewing, even without any accompanying words, can have impact. If it's so easy to offer such a gift to the audience, why withhold it?

There are numerous ways to structure a talk that can allow moments of visual indulgence that will significantly increase the audience's sense of delight, even when the topic itself isn't necessarily beautiful.

The designer and TED Fellow Lucy McRae packed dozens of intriguing, gorgeous images and videos into her talk, all of which generated their own sense of wonder — even when she was talking about body odor.

Likewise, the graphic style of a presentation, with elegant font choices, illustrations, and/or custom animations, can make it irresistible.

These are some core principles. But with visuals, the devil is in the details. To take us a little deeper, let me invite back to the page Tom Rielly, a man for whom bad visuals are a source of physical pain. Tom, over to you!

Tom Rielly writes:

Great! Let's start with the tools you'll use.

PRESENTATION SOFTWARE TIPS

As of 2016, there are three main presentation tools: PowerPoint, Keynote (for Mac), and Prezi. PowerPoint is ubiquitous, though I find Keynote easier to use, and with better typography and graphics. Prezi (in which TED was an early investor) offers an alternative mode in which, instead of a linear succession of slides, you move around a two-dimensional landscape, zooming in and out to focus on what matters to you.

Most projectors and screens these days are the dimensions of a modern widescreen television: 16:9, as opposed to the 4:3 of old TVs. Yet presentation software opens up in 4:3 mode. You want to immediately change the settings to 16:9 (unless you're speaking at a venue where they might still have only 4:3 projectors).

Don't use the software's built-in templates of bullets, letters, and dashes. Your presentation will look the same as everyone else's, and the templates end up being limiting. I recommend you start with a totally blank slide. If you're showing a lot of photos, use black as the background — it will disappear and your photos will pop.

Most photographs should be shown "full bleed." That's not a horror-movie term but an old printing term meaning that the image covers the entire screen. Better to have three full-bleed photos in a row than three on one slide. Photos are often still shot at 4:3, so if you wish to show a picture without cropping its top and bottom, put it on a black slide, which will leave unobtrusive black borders on the left and right.

Photo resolution: Use pictures with the highest resolution possible to avoid annoying pixelation of the images when projected on large screens. There is no such thing as too high a resolution, unless it slows the software down.

FONTS/TYPEFACES

It's usually best to use one typeface per presentation. Some typefaces are better suited than others. We usually recommend medium-weight sans-serif fonts like Helvetica or Arial. But don't use excessively thin fonts as they are hard to read, especially on a dark background. If in doubt, keep it simple.

Font size

Tiny type causes the audience to struggle. Use 24 points or larger in most cases. Use *at most* three sizes of your chosen typeface per presentation, and there should be a reason for each size. Large size is for titles/headlines; medium size is for your main ideas; small size is for supporting ideas.

Font background

If you're going to place type over a photo, make sure you place it where your audience can read it. If a photo is too busy to put type on directly, add a small black bar at the bottom and put the type on it.

Font color

Here the operative words are *simple* and *contrast*. Black on white, a dark color on white, and white or yellow on black all look good because they have great contrast and are easy to read. Use only one color of font per presentation unless you want to show emphasis or surprise. Never use a light-color type on a light-color background or dark-color type on a dark-color background — for example, light blue on yellow or red on black just won't be easy to read.

LEGIBILITY

After you make your font and color choices, look at your presentation on your computer or — way better — on your TV or a projector, and stand back 6 to 12 feet. Can you read everything? Do the photos look clear without pixelation? If not, readjust.

WHAT NOT TO DO

- Bullets belong in *The Godfather*. Avoid them at all costs.
- Dashes belong at the Olympics, not at the beginning of text.
- Resist underlining and italics — they're too hard to read. Bold typefaces are OK.
- Drop shadows can occasionally be useful to improve legibility, especially for type on top of photos, but use the effect sparingly.
- Don't use multiple type effects in the same line. It just looks terrible.

EXPLANATIONS AND DIAGRAMS

Use builds — add words and images to a slide through a series of clicks — to focus people's attention on one idea at a time. Give your audience enough time to absorb each step. Don't feed too much of the slide at a time or people will get overwhelmed.

PHOTO CREDITS

In the scientific community it's especially important to credit each photo on every slide. But it's better to avoid large type, because those citations will draw the audience's eye away from your slide. If all the images are from one source, you can say thanks to *National Geographic* out loud, or you can add one photo credit that says: "Photos courtesy of *National Geographic*," and then you don't have to repeat it on every slide.

If you do need to include credits, they should be positioned and styled consistently, in the same place, same font, same size (no more than 10 point) on every slide. And cut them down from "Photo Credit: Augustin Alvarez, Ames Research Center, NASA, Mountain View, CA" to "Augustin Alvarez, NASA." Note that some rights holders, such as museums, may resist abbreviating their credits. But it's worth asking. I usually set credits in white, reversed out of the image and rotated 90 degrees so they sit vertically, up the right side of the slide. Ask your friends: are the credits pulling focus away from the images? If so, they are too prominent.

PICTURES OF YOU AND YOUR TEAM

It's great to include a photo of you in your working environment: lab, bush, Large Hadron Collider. But resist including more than one unless there is a reason. Ben Saunders told us how he journeyed to the North and South Poles. His image is necessary in most photos to tell that story. There was also a whole team of people who worked tirelessly to make Ben's expedition possible, but to show photos of them would have taken the audience's focus away from the main story. While we understand that you want to share the credit, pictures of your team, especially in a yearbook-style compilation of individuals, matter to you but not to your audience. Resist, and if you must have one photo, make it an organic grouping. It's much better to depict your team in context during a presentation.

VIDEOS

Videos can be amazing tools to demonstrate your work and ideas. However, you should rarely show clips longer than 30 seconds. And in an 18-minute talk, show no more than two to four clips unless your work absolutely depends on it. It's best if video clips are of your work and you have rights to them (versus a clip from *Star Wars*); explain something that can't be explained by still images; and have great production value (shot in high-definition, with good lighting and especially good sound). A badly produced video will have your audience thinking more about its poor quality than about its content. Make sure it's organic and authentic, not produced by your PR department or with bombastic canned music. *Hint:* When you are working, capture video of everything, because you may decide to use it later, even if you don't know when. TED invests in high-quality video and photographs, and they just get more valuable as the years pass.

You can embed a video in your presentation, but remember to check with the A/V team to be sure it's definitely working before you go on stage.

TRANSITIONS

This is the dreaded quicksand of many a presenter. Rule of thumb: Avoid nearly all of them. Shimmer, sparkle, confetti, twirl, clothesline, swirl, cube, scale, swap, swoosh, fire explosions, and dropping and bouncing are all real Keynote transitions. And I never use any of them, except for humor and irony. They are gimmicky and serve to drop you out of your ideas and into the mechanics of your software. There are two transitions I do like: none (an instant cut, like in film editing) and dissolve. None (or cut) is great when you want an instant response to your clicker, and dissolve looks natural if it's set to a time interval of less than half a second. Cut and dissolve even have two subconscious meanings: With cut you're shifting to a new idea, and with dissolve the two slides are related in some way. That's not a hard and fast rule, but it's valid. You can use cuts and dissolves in the same presentation.

If there is no reason for a transition, don't use one. In summary, your transition should never call attention to itself.

TRANSPORTING FILES

Send your presentation to your hosts, and bring a USB stick with your complete presentation *and* your video, separate from your presentation. Also include the fonts used in the presentation. Even if I have sent a presentation in advance to the venue where I'll be speaking, I always bring it with me too. Important: Before sending over the Internet or copying to USB, put all these files into a folder and compress the folder into a .zip file. That will make sure that Keynote or PowerPoint will gather all the pieces of your presentation in one place. Do label each video clearly, including its location. For example, SIOBHAN STEPHENS SLIDE 12: VIDEO: MOTH EMERGES FROM COCOON.

RIGHTS

Make sure you have a legal license to use the photos, videos, music, and any special fonts, or that they are in the Creative Commons or outright free to use. It's always easiest and best to use your own work. If you use a Whitney Houston song, for example, it could cost thousands of dollars to clear it for use in your live talk and especially online.

TESTING

There are two kinds of testing: human and technical. First, for human testing, I recommend that you test your presentation — especially your slides — on family or friends who are not in your field. Ask them afterwards what they understood, what they didn't, and what further questions they have. Testing is extremely important, especially on very technical or abstruse subjects.

Equally important is technical testing. I bought a Kensington remote for $35 that plugs into my computer's USB so I can click through the talk as I would on stage. Are the slides crisp and bright? Are the transitions quick enough? Are the fonts correct? Do the videos play OK? Are there any technical glitches of any kind? Running through your talk a lot will help you know if it is reliable.

Always ask what kind of computer will be used to show your presentation, if it can be shown in the same program and with the same fonts you used to create it, and, if your host is using the same software, ask what version they are using.

Make sure you use the very latest version of the software because that's generally what organizers will have, and onsite conversions from one version to another are stressful and sometimes require lots of finessing. Once, I created a presentation in Keynote on a Mac and it was imported into PowerPoint on a PC. It looked like a disaster in rehearsal. I convinced them to get a Mac and Keynote and it worked great.

Never give a presentation unless you have walked through your slides — and especially videos — on the equipment that will actually be used to show them. It's particularly important to get the sound person to check the sound levels of any audio in your presentation, especially if you plan to speak over it. Inaudibility or a startling burst of sound will throw you off.

WORKING WITH DESIGNERS

Most people can learn to make good slides, but if the stakes are high and budget permits, by all means enlist the help of a presentation graphics designer. Notice how I didn't say just any designer. Someone who focuses on websites or printed materials may not be as fluid with the art and grammar of conveying ideas through slides. Ask for previous work. You can find them on Behance and other websites.

Four more important points:

1. Even if you have a corporate graphics department to do the work, you should be involved from the beginning. Be proactive. Don't just review the finished video; make sure you are present and participating. Most designers are great at what they do, but they're helping you express yourself, so it just makes sense to be involved.

2. If you are uncomfortable with someone else's slide recommendations, trust your instincts. It's you up there on stage, after all.

3. We work with a lot of designers remotely, using Skype, email, and Dropbox, and it works well. There is no reason your designers have to be nearby.

4. Help doesn't need to be expensive. For presentation graphics, I like to work with small design shops of just one to about fifteen people because I get to work more with the principals. There is also a steady supply of recent art and design school graduates from places like RISD, Art Center College of Design, Pratt, Art Institutes, Cooper Union, and many more colleges around the world.

VERSION CONTROL

Use version control religiously, and a tool like Dropbox to store all your drafts as well as your fonts, photos, videos, and sound. It's always a good idea to name files with the version number, your name, the venue, and later the TED session, if you know it. For example, like this: v4trjwTomRiellyPrezTED2016 Session11. The initials ("trjw") tell who worked on it last. *Hint:* Put the version number and last person's initials at the beginning of the file name, otherwise you might not be able to tell easily which is which. Every time you pass it to or fro, save a new version with a new number, and before you share the Dropbox link with the production team at an event, make a folder inside Dropbox for the old versions and keep the latest version separate. Mark the final version "FINAL" at the beginning or end of the filename.

Your designer will love you if you or a team member assemble as many of the assets (photos, videos, sounds) as possible in a folder before he starts designing. Also, to help the designer, sometimes I'll open a new Keynote file and make dummy slides with instructions, for example: *This slide will show one of the species we're trying to conserve. This slide will show the dry lakebed;* etc.

Do that for as many slides as you can, arrange them, and send the file to the designer. This is the equivalent of a filmmaker's Post-it Notes on the wall — they help her organize her ideas.

Finally, as in all things with graphics, less is more.

And back to Chris:

A round of applause for Tom, please!

And finally, if you want to see state of the art in action, here are three more speakers whose visuals we adore.

The glorious images shown by conservation photographer Mac Stone at TEDxUC fully justify the title of his talk, "Photos that make you want to save the Everglades."

At TEDxVancouver, Jer Thorp spoke of the impact of clear infographics and proved his point with countless examples.

And at TEDxSydney, biomedical animator Drew Barry used astounding 3D animations to reveal hidden processes in our cells.

Once you have a plan for your visuals, it's time to go back to the words, and then figure out how you will turn them into an actual talk. There are two quite different approaches here, and, as we'll see, the world's best speakers disagree strongly on this topic. Happily, there's a way to bridge the divide.

11
SCRIPTING
To Memorize or Not to Memorize?

At a recent TED conference we had invited a brilliant up-and-coming physicist to give a talk about remarkable new developments in the field. He had a reputation as his university's finest science speaker. His lectures were always packed because of his gift for making the complex plain, the obscure exciting. And in rehearsal he wowed us with his passion and eloquence and clarity. I was so looking forward to his big moment.

He started out well, striding the stage and offering up an intriguing metaphor that the capacity audience was enjoying getting its head around. And then . . . the first glitch. He lost his way for a moment. He smiled and asked for a moment, pulled out his iPhone and reminded himself where he was. Then he moved on. No problem. Except it happened again 40 seconds later. The metaphor was starting to get impossibly convoluted. People were scratching their heads and starting to feel stressed for him. You could hear his voice starting to tighten. He coughed. I handed him a bottle of water. For a moment it seemed to help. But no. In horrifying slow motion, the talk imploded in front of us. As comedian Julia Sweeney later remarked, it was as if he was disappearing into one of the black holes he was talking about. Out came the phone again two, three, four more times. He began reading from it. The smile and passion had gone. The entire water bottle had been downed. Beads of sweat were glistening on his forehead. He sounded like he was choking to death. He somehow got to the end, to a round of awkward, sympathetic applause.

His talk was the talk of the conference. But not in the way he had dreamed it would be.

Here's the thing. This wasn't his fault. It was mine. In preparing him, I had encouraged him to take the time to create a truly blockbuster talk and to script it out carefully in advance. It was the approach most TED speakers used, and it seemed to be working well in rehearsal. But it wasn't his natural speaking style. He had explained that topic masterfully to countless classes of students using fluent, in-the-moment language that came straight out of his amazing brain. I should have asked him to bring that skill to TED. (In fact, he *did* bring that skill to TED. Just the prior day he had come on stage to give a brilliant, off-the-cuff explanation of a major breaking story in Physics. It was the scripting that messed him up.)

There are many ways to prepare for and deliver a talk, and it's important to find the one that's right for you. Because when it comes to the exact moment, even if you've prepared something that is stunning, there is a long list of things that can go wrong, among them:

- Your tone of voice puts your audience to sleep.
- You sound like you're reciting.
- You run out of time before you've completed half of what you wanted to say.
- You get flustered trying to remember how your slides fit with the words you prepared.
- Your videos fail to start, and your slide clicker doesn't work properly.
- You fail to make eye contact with a single member of the audience.

- You feel uncomfortable on stage, not knowing whether you should walk around a little or stay rooted to one spot. So instead you compromise and shuffle awkwardly from leg to leg.
- The audience fails to laugh when they were supposed to.
- The audience laughs when they most definitely *were not* supposed to.
- The standing ovation you dreamed of is replaced by a smattering of polite applause.
- And — the one thing people dread most — you forget what you were going to say next, your mind goes blank, and you freeze.

Happily, with diligent preparation, the risk of any of these happening can be truly minimized. But as the story above illustrates, it has to be the right type of preparation. And that begins with knowing *how* you plan to deliver your talk. Different speakers take very different approaches. In this chapter we'll try to help you figure out what approach is best for you.

Some years ago, TED used to be quite rigid in its rules on talk delivery: *No lecterns. Never read your talk.* And, in general, those rules make sense. People truly respond to the vulnerability of a speaker who stands there unprotected by a lectern and speaks from the heart. That is human-to-human communication in its purest form.

But there is also power in variety. If every speaker stood in the center of the stage, enunciating with thrilling clarity a perfectly memorized talk, it would soon get tiresome. When a group of people goes away for a week to a conference, the speakers who have the most impact are often those who do things differently. If everyone is speaking without a script, the quirky professor who sidles out to a lectern and mischievously *reads* his talk may well be the one who is remembered.

And more than anything else, what matters is that speakers are comfortable and confident, giving the talk in the way that best allows them to focus on what they're passionate about.

We discovered this when we invited the Nobel laureate Daniel Kahneman to TED. Known as the father of behavioral economics, he's an extraordinary thinker with a toolkit of ideas that can change any worldview. We had originally asked him to speak in the traditional TED way. No lectern. Just stand on the stage, with some note cards if need be, and give the talk. But in rehearsal, it was clear that he was uncomfortable. He hadn't been able to fully memorize the talk and so kept pausing and glancing down awkwardly to catch himself up.

Finally I said to him, "Danny, you've given thousands of talks in your time. How are you most comfortable speaking?" He said he liked to put his computer on a lectern so that he could refer to his notes more readily. We tried that, and he relaxed immediately. But he was also looking down at the screen a little too much. The deal we struck was to give him the lectern in return for looking out at the audience as much as he could. And that's exactly what he did. His excellent talk did not come across as a recited or read speech at all. It felt connected. And he said everything he wanted to say, with no awkwardness.

So today, we don't have set rules. We just have suggestions for helping speakers find the mode of delivery that will be most powerful for them.

One of the first key decisions you need to make — and ideally you'll make it early on in your talk preparation — is whether you will:

A. write out the talk in full as a complete script (to be read, memorized, or a combination of the two), or
B. have a clearly worked-out structure and speak in the moment to each of your points.

There are powerful arguments in favor of each strategy.

SCRIPTED TALKS

The huge advantage of going the scripted route is that you can make the best possible use of your available time. It can be incredibly hard to condense all you want to say into 10, 15, or 18 minutes. If there are tricky explanations involved, or important steps in your persuasion process, it may be essential for you to get every word down and tweak every sentence and paragraph to perfection. Scripting also has the advantage that drafts of the talk can be shared ahead of time. We love it when speakers send us a draft a couple of months ahead of the conference. That allows us time to give feedback on which elements might be cut and which might need further explanation.

But the big drawback of a script is that, unless you deliver it in the right way, the talk may not feel fresh. Being read to and being spoken to are two very different experiences. In general (and there are exceptions), audiences respond far more powerfully to the latter. This is something of a puzzle. If they're the same words, and everyone present knows they were written by the speaker, why should we care how they are delivered to us?

It may be because human-to-human communication is a dynamic process, unfolding in real time. You say something. I look at your eyes and make all manner of unconscious judgments. Is this something you really mean? Are you passionate about it? Are you committed to it? As a listener, until I know these things, it's too risky to open up my mind to you. That means there's huge power to watching someone "think out loud" in the moment. We can sense your conviction, and we get to be part of the excitement of seeing a big idea identified, battled with, and finally shaken into shape. The fact that we can sense that you truly *mean* what you're saying in the moment helps give us permission to embrace that meaning.

By contrast, when the words are read, they may feel impersonal and distanced. It's a bit like watching a sports event on DVR. The game has already been won or lost. Even when we don't know the outcome, we don't care quite as much. (And imagine how much worse that DVR experience would be if we sensed that the commentary had been added after the game and was being read, not evoked in real time. That's how read talks can sound.)

So if you go the script route, you have three main strategies open to you:

1. Know the talk so well that it doesn't for a moment *sound* scripted. (More on this shortly.)
2. Refer to the script (either from a lectern — preferably not one that blocks out your whole body — or possibly from a screen or confidence monitor), but compensate by looking up during each sentence to make eye contact with the audience. Notice I didn't say to *read* the script. You may have the entire thing there in front of you, but it's important that you feel as if you're in speaking mode, not reading mode. The audience can tell the difference. It's all about giving meaning to the words as you speak as naturally and passionately as you can. It's about audience eye contact and smiles or other facial expressions. It's about being familiar enough with the script that you're really just glancing down once every sentence or two. Yes, this takes work, but it's worth it, and it's still far less daunting than full memorization.
3. Condense the script to bullet points and plan to express each point in your own language in the moment. This has its own set of challenges, covered below in Unscripted Talks.

There are only two circumstances where you might get away with actually reading your script:

1. Your talk is accompanied by absolutely gorgeous images or videos that play while you are speaking. In this scenario, you are the lyrical caption provider. The audience's attention is on the screen. Photographer James Nachtwey's TED Prize talk was like this.
2. You are a truly great writer, and the audience understands that they are listening to a piece of written work. But, as we'll see below, even for great writers with a script in lyrical language, it can be more powerful *not* to read.

Despite these caveats, for the majority of speakers, the most reliable way to say what you really want to say in the most powerful way is to first script it out and get to know it so it's part of you. But that is hard work. For most of us, an 18-minute talk can easily take five or six hours to memorize. An hour a day for a week. If you don't have that time available, don't even try to go this route. When you show up on stage, you really don't want to be struggling to remember a script.

When that happens, the problem is not so much the risk of the total freeze. It's that the audience can *tell* you're reciting. They may see your eyes roll around between paragraphs as you bring the next sentence to mind. More likely they will notice that your tone is slightly flat and robotic, because you are focused on bringing the right sentences out instead of bringing real meaning to those sentences.

This is actually something of a tragedy. You put in all that work to create an amazing talk, but then never really gave it a chance to have impact.

This problem is fixable. But it takes some effort.

Imagine you get to observe a friend who, over the course of a week or so, tries to memorize his talk. Let's say that you ask him every day to give the best version of the talk that he can without using notes. You would notice something odd: Early on in the process, he would be quite convincing (if a little unstructured). He doesn't actually know any of the talk by heart yet, so he simply does his best to give you the information he knows in approximately the order he's planned.

But a few days into the process, you notice a change. He has reached the point where he knows quite a bit of the talk by heart, and so those parts come out in eloquent paragraphs. *But,* you don't feel the same original liveliness from them. You feel his stress. You hear words like, *Let's see; Just a minute; Let me start that again.* Or you simply hear those paragraphs rattled off a little robotically.

Those clues are giveaways that the talk is being recited rather than spoken with meaning. I call this phase of preparation the *Uncanny Valley.* It's a term borrowed from a phenomenon in computer animation where the technology of animating humanlike characters is super-close to seeming real but is not *quite* there. The effect is creepy: worse than if the animator had steered clear of realism altogether. If your speaker friend comes to the stage in this mode, his talk will probably fail. He'd do better to forget about delivering a scripted talk and instead write down seven bullet points and speak a bit about each of them. Or take the script with him to the stage.

But if he persists in the memorization process, by the sixth or seventh day, you will notice a thrilling change. Suddenly the speaker really knows the talk. He knows it so well that recalling it is a snap. Suddenly your friend can use his conscious attention to focus on the meaning of the words once again.

So what I'd say to speakers planning to memorize their talks is this: *That's great. You're giving yourself the best chance for a huge hit. But it is absolutely essential that you take yourself through Un-*

canny Valley and don't get stuck there. *If you're not willing to commit to do that, do not memorize!*

And how should you memorize? TED speakers use lots of different methods. Pamela Meyer, who gave a hit talk on how to detect a liar, appeared to be speaking honestly with this advice:

> At Camp Seafarer in North Carolina, we had to tread water while singing camp songs. Then, to make it harder, we had to tread water while also wiggling our forefingers in complicated patterns to the beat of the song. You haven't really memorized your talk thoroughly until you can do an entire other activity that requires mental energy *while* giving your talk. Can you give your talk while measuring out the ingredients to make brownies? Can you give your talk while filing all the messy papers on your desk into a file cabinet? If you can give your talk while the cognitive load is that high on your system, you can give it well while focused on stage.

Watch Pam's talk. Does it sound memorized? It does not. It sounds completely natural.

TED speaker and voice artist Rives agrees with her advice:

> When I have time to memorize a talk, I memorize the $#@! out of it. I memorize the talk until the talk is like a tune. I workshop the talk in my mouth. I run it fast and slow, singsong and stentorian, cool and cooler. I rehearse the talk until I'm performing the talk, not remembering it. And good riddance, reciting. My personal memorization ritual usually happens the night(s) before my talk, in a hotel room. I turn on a TV interview show, slightly louder than usual, to create maximum cognitive interference. Then (no kidding) I hold one leg behind me and recite my talk to my reflection in the mirror. If I stop smiling, I have to start over. If I stall out, I have to start over. If I survive one entire recitation, I won't forget my talk and the smiles will happen as they may.

If you drive a lot, you could consider recording the talk (just read it into your smartphone, for example) and then playing it back on low volume, while you try to speak just ahead of it. Then try again with the speed accelerated (most phones can do this). One of TED's favorite speaker coaches, Gina Barnett, believes the key is to be able to recite the talk at double speed. When you can do that comfortably, giving the talk at normal speed will be automatic and you can focus 100 percent on meaning. She also has a wonderful insight into how to think of memorization. "This is what I tell people: Practice doesn't make perfect. *Practice makes imperfection livable.* Because when you know something inside out, you can PLAY with what comes your way, rather than shut it out."

So that's the key. Don't think of it as *reciting* the talk. You're supposed to *live* it. Embody it. Your sole goal is to get to the point where remembering the words is no longer an effort and you can use your stage time to impart passion and meaning to the audience. *It must come across as if you are sharing these ideas for the first time.*

It can be done. Not every speaking occasion justifies this kind of time investment. But for those that do, it's truly worth it.

One other key question for scripted talks is what type of language you should use. Spoken language or written language? The language we use in everyday speech is quite different from the language writers use. More direct, less lyrical.

The advice of most speaking coaches is to stick rigidly to spoken language. That way it can be spoken from the heart, in the moment. It is, after all, a *talk* not a *write*. Martin Luther King didn't say, "Vivid, powerful, unforgettable is the vision I bring to you this day." He said, "I have a dream."

Harvard professor Dan Gilbert advises his students to speak their talks into a recorder first, then transcribe them, and use that as the initial draft of their talk. Why? "Because when people write, they tend to use words, phrases, sentence structures, and cadences that no one uses in natural speech. So when you start with written text and then try to adapt it for performance, you are basically trying to turn one form of communication into another, and odds are that your alchemy will fail."

And many other speakers, as we'll see, believe the best way to "write" a talk is simply to try to speak it out loud multiple times.

But, once again, it's a mistake to be too rigid about this. Great writers can make a different type of talk, one in which the elegant prewritten language is the whole point.

Take a look at this paragraph from a memorable talk at TED2014 by Andrew Solomon:

> We don't seek the painful experiences that hew our identities, but we seek our identities in the wake of painful experiences. We cannot bear a pointless torment, but we can endure great pain if we believe that it's purposeful. Ease makes less of an impression on us than struggle. We could have been ourselves without our delights, but not without the misfortunes that drive our search for meaning.

Solomon is an extraordinary writer, and it shows. This is language that would naturally appear in a book or magazine feature, not language that you would naturally use in a one-to-one conversation with a friend at a bar. The clues are in the language's lyricism — words like *hew* and *torment*. This is a powerful piece of *writing,* and it's meant to be heard that way. Even though he was speaking from notes, the lyrical power of the language made us feel we were in the hands of a master craftsman. We *wanted* the talk to have been prewritten. (By the way, Andrew told me that this actually *is* how he speaks to friends at bars. I wish I could be a bystander.)

Talks like Andrew's can be read. Perhaps they *should* be read. But if you go this route, even if you're a truly great writer, do your audience the honor of *knowing your script* so well that you can still give a sense of *feeling* it in the moment. Mean every sentence. Look up as often as you can and make eye contact. And perhaps, if you want to add a moment of powerful impact toward the end, abandon your script before the last page. Walk away from the lectern, toss away your notes, move to the front of the stage, and speak the conclusion directly from the heart.

UNSCRIPTED TALKS

This term covers a large landscape, from impromptu ad-libbing to intricately prepared and structured talks accompanied by rich visuals. What they all have in common is that, in the moment of delivery, you are not trying to recall a specific prewritten sentence. Instead you are thinking about the subject matter and looking for the best words to convey the point at hand. At most, you have a set of notes to guide you through the main elements of the talk.

There's a lot to be said for going unscripted. It can sound fresh, alive, real, like you are thinking out loud. If this is your most comfortable speaking style, and if you are covering material that is very familiar to you, this may be your best choice.

But it is important to distinguish *unscripted* from *unprepared*. In an important talk, there's no excuse for the latter. Many unscripted talks, alas, result in half-baked explanations, non sequiturs, key elements missed, and rambling overruns.

So how do you prepare for an unscripted talk? A lot will depend on what type of journey you plan to take the audience on. A talk built around a single story will be a lot easier than one where you're trying to construct a complex explanation or a nuanced argument. But the key to the process is to go back to the metaphor of the journey and ask yourself what each step of the journey looks like. At a minimum, a label for each step can be your set of bullet points or mental notes.

You also need a strategy to avoid the obvious pitfalls of such an approach:

1. *That suddenly you can't, in the moment, find the words to explain a key concept.* Antidote: Practice out loud several versions of each step in your journey until you're confident that you have complete mental clarity around each one.

2. *That you leave out something crucial.* It may be worth working on a transition from each step to the next that makes the sequence come naturally. Perhaps you commit to remembering those transition phrases, or add them to your notes.

3. *That you overrun your time slot.* This is upsetting to conference organizers, and to all the speakers who follow you. It can also stress out your audience. Don't do it. The only antidotes are to A. Try out the talk several times to be sure it can indeed be done within the time limit. If not, you must cut material. B. Be disciplined about watching the clock and know how far you need to be when half of your time has gone by. C. Prepare a talk that is no more than 90 percent of your time limit.

One temptation many speakers fall prey to is to use their slides as crutches. In the worst form, this means a series of dismal slides covered with text and bullet points that the speaker works through laboriously. Most people by now understand that this is a truly terrible way to give a talk. Every word you speak that someone has already seen on a slide is a word that carries zero punch. It's not news anymore.

A well-structured set of slides can boost your confidence in keeping the talk moving along, but it needs to be done subtly. For example, you could have a new image that links thematically to each element in your talk. If you get stuck, advance to the next slide and it should pull you back on track. But note that this is not ideal. Elegant timing of slide transitions can add a lot to a talk's impact. You should often aim to tease the arrival of a slide before revealing it. *And that brings us to the future of cities* [click], is much more powerful than [click] *Ah, yes. Next I want to talk about the future of cities.*

Frankly, the old-fashioned method of a set of punchy notes handwritten on cards is still a decent way to keep yourself on track. Use the words that will trigger a key sentence or a phrase that launches the next step in your talk.

One thing to understand is that audiences really don't mind one bit if you pause your talk for a moment to take stock. You might feel some discomfort. They won't. The key is to be relaxed about it. When superstar DJ Mark Ronson came to TED2014, he was masterful at this. He lost his way at one point, but he simply smiled, walked over to a bottle of water, sipped it, told the audience this was his memory crutch, studied his notes, sipped again, and by the time he got going again, everyone liked him even more.

TED speakers have widely different opinions, by the way, on whether a memorized script or a prepared talk-in-the-moment is the better way to go.

Author Elizabeth Gilbert is firmly in the former camp.

I always memorize my talks — or at least I come as close to complete memorization as I am capable. Memorization makes me feel comfortable and safe; improvisation makes me feel chaotic and exposed. Public speaking, even for those of us who enjoy it, can be frightening, and fear can make you go blank. But when I have worked hard to memorize a speech, just as if it were a poem or a song, then I can simply stand there and recite it, even as my conscious mind is blanking out. I would rather risk sounding like I am reciting something from memory than sounding like I lost my way, or like I never had a plan, or like I have no idea what the heck I'm talking about up there. During my first TED Talk, I was so nervous and agitated that my conscious mind was flat-out not working at all for the first 5 minutes on stage. Thankfully, though, my deep-brain memory and my mouth still worked, so the words just came spilling out exactly as I had rehearsed them. As the minutes ticked by, and as I fell into the familiar groove of my talk, I was able to slowly relax and warm up, and by the middle of the speech, I was actually enjoying myself and improvising a bit. But the strict memorization was what kept me safe during that opening bout of nerves. Therefore, I have come to think of memorization as something like a soldier's combat training; when the moment of battle comes, you want to be operating by instinct, not by conscious thought.

Amanda Palmer agrees:

I'm a master improviser, but talks aren't the place for improvising, especially on a stage like TED where the time limit is so strict. I considered leaving spots where I could let myself muse and waffle a bit, but as I wrote and rewrote and practiced, I realized that I could convey MUCH more meaning if I did the work ahead of time and distilled my 40-second waffle down into a bite-sized, 5-second protein pill.

Pam Meyer told me the reason to script a talk is so that you can make sure every sentence counts:

You know how when you give a talk, you like certain parts more than others? You have to love every single sentence. You actually have to go through your script and your slides and ask the question, "Is this essential to advancing my message, and is this interesting, really interesting? Do I love saying this line?" and put every single sentence and slide through the test. If anything lands in the maybe pile . . . it's out.

Salman Khan has a different stance:

Believing what you are saying in real time has a much larger impact than saying the exact right words. I personally tend to list out bullet points of what I want to talk about and then try communicating those ideas in my natural language as if I'm talking to friends at a dinner table. The key is to keep your mind focused on the ideas and let the words fall out. The audience knows when you are thinking about what you are saying versus when you have just memorized a script.

Steven Johnson agrees.

In all of my TED Talks, I very deliberately did not memorize them, precisely because the audience can hear memorized text very clearly, and it takes away from the spontaneous, engaged nature of speaking to a live audience. The other problem with a memorized speech is that when it fails, it fails catastrophically. If you're just talking, following a rough outline, if you slip up a bit and forget a small piece, it's barely noticeable to anyone but you. But if you're reciting something from memory and draw a blank, you're likely to freeze with nowhere to go. It's like your mental teleprompter has frozen.

One of the world's most talented speakers, Sir Ken Robinson, is also in this camp. He told me that several parts of his blockbuster TED Talk on creativity were improvised in the moment.

People should do whatever makes them comfortable on stage and helps them to relax. If memorizing works, they should do that. It doesn't for me. One of my priorities in giving a talk is to establish a personal relationship with the audience, and to do that I want room to improvise. Whether it's ten people or ten thousand, a seminar or a rally, I feel it's essential to talk with people, not at them, and to be authentic in doing it. I do plan talks carefully, however. When I walk on stage, I always know what I want to have said before I walk off again. But I also want to connect with these people in this room today. It doesn't matter how many rooms I've spoken in before, today's audience is always new and different.

Meanwhile, Dan Gilbert thinks it's not either/or. First of all he writes a script for his talks (being careful to use spoken English).

But then, when I deliver them, I don't stick to the script I wrote. So why do I write them? Because writing a story is how you find out where the holes are! A great talk is both scripted AND improvisational. It is precisely like a great jazz performance: First, the opening and closing are always completely scripted; second, the general structure is fully determined before the first horn blows; but third, what makes jazz interesting and captivating is that in the middle of a tune there is always some point (or several points) in which the player can go off script and spontaneously create something that captures the mood of that particular audience in that particular room at that particular moment in time. The player can take a few moments to do this, but he must always know when to come home, and he must always know where home is. A totally improvisational talk is like free jazz: an utter abomination almost every time it happens. A totally scripted talk is like a classical music concert: intricate, deep, and flawlessly executed, but often predictable enough to put the audience to sleep because they know from the start that there will be no surprises.

And ad guru Rory Sutherland also recommends the best of both worlds:

Churchill, I think, said this—"Rehearse your impromptu re-marks." Or at least leave room in your talk for a few optional asides. If everything in a talk leads in perfect lockstep fashion toward its conclusion, it wins points for logic but can leave the audience feeling as though they have been on a forced march rather than a pleasant, companionable walk.

Here's the bottom line: The majority of TED speakers do in fact script their whole talk and memorize it, and they do their best to avoid letting it *sound* memorized. If you have time to do that, and to work your way past the robotic Uncanny Valley, it probably gives you your best shot at encapsulating all you want to say *and* avoiding the usual traps of a memorized talk. But if you don't have the time to truly memorize until the talk is second na-ture, or if you already know that's just not how you give a great talk, please don't go this route.

The key is to find the mode you can feel confident about, and commit to it.

If that choice seems a little stressful, here's some good news: As you start to rehearse, the difference between the two modes starts to fade. The starting points may be different, but in both cases you end up with a talk that is meticulously prepared and passion-ately delivered.

12

RUN-THROUGHS

Wait, I Need to Rehearse?

Whichever mode of speaking you decide on, there's a very simple, very obvious tool you can use to improve your talk, but it's one that most speakers rarely undertake: *Rehearse. Repeatedly.*

Musicians rehearse before playing. Actors rehearse before opening the theater doors to the paying public. For public talks, the stakes may well be as high or higher than any concert or play, yet many speakers seem to think they can just walk on the stage and get it right the first time. Thus it is that, time and again, hundreds of people in the audience have to suffer countless minutes of needless pain simply because one person didn't prepare adequately. 'Tis a crying shame.

The greatest corporate communicator of recent times, Steve Jobs, didn't get there by talent alone. He put in hours of meticulous rehearsal for every major product launch Apple did. He obsessed over every detail.

Most of the big TED hits happened only because of the hours of prep the speakers put in. Jill Bolte Taylor, whose talk about her stroke exploded across the Internet in 2008, told me:

> I practiced literally hundreds of hours. Over and over again, even in my sleep as I would awake and find myself reciting the talk. Because the piece was so emotional for me, I would relive the morning of the stroke every time I shared the story. Because my emotion was authentic, the story was perceived as authentic, and we took the journey together.

Stem cell scientist Susan Solomon is equally passionate about the power of rehearsal:

> By the time you are ready to give your talk, you should have rehearsed it so many times that you feel as if you could do it in your sleep, and in front of any audience. Rehearse in front of friends. Rehearse by yourself. Rehearse with your eyes closed. Rehearse walking in the garden. Rehearse sitting at your desk, but without using your notes. And be sure that, in your rehearsals, you include your visuals, since timing with them is critical.

Rachel Botsman says you should take care with whom you practice:

> Practice your speech in front of someone who knows nothing about your work. I made the mistake of running through mine with people who are very familiar with me and what I am doing. The best feedback will be from people who can tell you where there are gaps in your narrative or where you are making assumptions that people will know x, y, z.

Self-professed introvert Susan Cain credits her rehearsal audience for significant improvements to her talk:

> I took TED's advice to heart: If you're going to memorize your talk, make sure you know it so well that the words come from the heart. It's not enough to practice it in front of the mirror or while you're walking the dog. Use a real stage, and speak to at least one audience member. The Friday night just before my talk, the amazing Wharton professor Adam Grant gathered an audience of his thirty top students and alums, and I gave my talk to them. Their feedback was so insightful that I stayed up all night to rewrite the final third of the talk. Then I had to spend the rest of the weekend re-memorizing. I don't advise waiting until the last minute like this! But I do recommend working with a real audience and a sage friend like Adam.

But here's a surprise. Even speakers who *don't* believe in scripting and memorizing their talks have still made a big point of rehearsing. Here's education reformer Salman Khan:

Deliver the speech at least five times in your bedroom, paraphrasing the core ideas. Even if you mess up or forget something, force yourself to finish with each go (and always keep time). In my mind, the value of practice is less about memorization than about making you comfortable and less stressed. If you are confident and at ease, everyone will have a better time.

Science writer Mary Roach concurs:

My talk was not written out word for word or memorized. But it was rehearsed — at least twenty-five times, using ten note cards and a timer. There's a kind of unintentional memorization that develops naturally from repetition. I think that's what you're after. Memorization feels safer, but a little risk is good. Fear is energy, and you want some of that running through your wires.

That phrase *unintentional memorization* is an important one. If you rehearse enough, you may find yourself simply knowing the talk in its best form. When Clay Shirky came to the TED offices to give a talk about a ballooning controversy regarding copyright legislation, I marveled at his ability to smoothly deliver the whole complicated thing without a script, without notes even. I asked him how he did it. Answer: Repeated rehearsals. But rehearsals that actually *created* the talk. Here's what he said:

I once heard Ron Vawter, the greatest actor I've ever known, answer a question about his rehearsal technique. He replied, "I just say the words enough times that they sound like they're coming from me." That's what I do — I prepare for a talk by talking. I start with a basic idea, figure out an introductory sentence or two, and then just imagine myself explaining it to people who care about the idea.

In the beginning, the talking is to get a sense of what fits and doesn't fit — it's more editing than rehearsing. In that TED Talk I had a whole bit about scarcity in industries other than TV, but it kept feeling awkward to cram it in, so I dropped it. After a while, the talking becomes for pacing and timing. And by the end, I'm mostly just talking out the transitions. Slides help, of course, but rehearsing the transitions is especially important. The audience needs to hear in your voice when you're doubling down on an idea, versus when you're changing subjects.

I always make written notes, but I never write out the talk — talks shouldn't feel like writing read aloud. Instead, I write down a list of what theater people call beats: here's a thought about the DMCA, then one about SOPA, then one about the DNS, and so on. I make the last list of these beats just before I go on stage, as a last head-clearing reminder.

If you pull together the advice from Cain, Khan, Roach, and Shirky, you will see that the gap between memorized and in-the-moment talks starts to fade. The best memorized talks are known so well that speakers can concentrate on their *passion* for the ideas they contain. The best in-the-moment talks have been practiced enough times that their speakers know exactly what trajectory they should take, and they find many of the most powerful phrases already there in mind.

What we're really talking about here is not two different ways of *delivering* a talk, but rather, it's two different ways of *constructing* a talk. Some people start with a script, others with a set of bullet points, but the process of rehearsal moves these much closer together. In both cases, the goal is a carefully structured talk, delivered with in-the-moment focus.

Maybe, at this point, you'll push back and say that you hate talks that are rehearsed. You can always tell, however effortless someone thinks they're making it seem. *Talks should be fresh, unique, live!*

I know maybe a tiny handful of speakers who can do that. They're building on a lifetime of experience and/or an unusual ability to construct and focus an idea in real time. But for most of us, giving a talk "fresh" brings with it terrible tradeoffs: lack of focus, missed key points, lack of clarity, and time overrun, just to name a few. I really don't recommend this approach. When people think a talk sounds rehearsed, the problem is not *too much* rehearsal, it's *too little* rehearsal. The speaker is stuck in the Uncanny Valley.

But let's acknowledge this: Rehearsals are hard. They're inherently stressful. Even committing to a run-through out loud in your bedroom is hard. There may be some speaking occasions where you simply can't justify taking the time to do this (in which case, speaking from a hand-held set of bullet points, or from a script that you look up from as much as you can, are your best options). But if a talk is important, you really, really owe it to yourself and the audience to work through that stress by rehearsing. In doing that the stress starts to become replaced by confidence, and then by excitement.

Author Tracy Chevalier overcame her reluctance to rehearse and discovered how it can actually shape the talk.

> TED organizers place a lot of emphasis on rehearsing. They told me to practice so often I got annoyed. I have given many public talks and never practiced the way TED expected me to. In the end, however, I did rehearse, and was very glad of it. Most talks are not timed so tightly, and my style is often conversational and tangential. Practicing makes you realize just how much waffle there is in most talks. Practice, time yourself, and start cutting out all the asides and unnecessary stuff. I also found that in saying it aloud, I came up with phrases that worked well. I memorized those, then used them as anchors, or landing pads to touch down on. I didn't memorize the whole

talk — that can sound pretty fake unless you're an actor — but I did memorize the structure and those few landing pad phrases, and that made the talk tighter and better.

Even Bill Gates, one of the world's busiest men, puts a huge effort into learning and rehearsing his TED Talks. Once upon a time he was considered a poor public speaker. By taking preparation seriously, he's turned that around and has produced powerful talks on public health, energy, and education.

If it's worth Bill Gates's time and Susan Cain's time and Tracy Chevalier's time and Salman Khan's time to rehearse for a major talk, it's probably worth your time too.

Some things to ask your audience during or after these rehearsals:

- Did I get your attention from the get-go?
- Was I making eye contact?
- Did the talk succeed in building a new idea for you?
- Was each step of the journey satisfying?
- Were there enough examples to make everything clear?
- How was my tone of voice? Did it sound conversational (usually good) or as if I was preaching (usually bad)?
- Was there enough variety of tone and pacing?
- Did I sound as if I was reciting the talk?
- Were the attempts at humor natural or a little awkward? Was there enough humor?
- How were the visuals? Did they help or get in the way?
- Did you notice any annoying traits? Was I clicking my tongue? Swallowing too often? Shifting from side to side? Repeatedly using a phrase like "you know" or (worse) "like"?
- Were my body gestures natural?

- Did I finish on time?
- Were there moments you got a little bored? Was there something I could cut?

I recommend you have someone record these rehearsals on a smartphone so that you can take a look at yourself in action. You may immediately notice some physical trait that you're completely unconscious of that you'd prefer wasn't there.

Finally, let's talk about time limits. It's really important that you take the clock seriously. This is certainly true when you're part of a packed program. Overrunning the clock is stealing time from the speakers who follow you. But it's not just about avoiding upsetting them and the event organizer. It's also about landing your best talk. In our crazy modern attention economy, people respond to crisp, powerful content. They have no patience for flab. And it's not just a modern phenomenon. In history, many of the most powerful talks were short and to the point. Abraham Lincoln's Gettysburg Address clocked in at just over 2 minutes. The speaker before him droned on for 2 hours; what he said is long forgotten.

When it comes to the actual day, the last thing you want is to be worried about time. To avoid this, use your rehearsals to fine-tune your talk. You should plan to cut your material until you're sure you can finish well under the limit. This will allow time for audience laughter and a wee glitch or two. On the day itself, if you know you're going to be OK on time, it will allow you to focus 100 percent on the topic you should be focused on: explaining with passion the idea you care so much about.

Spoken word artist Rives has a nice guideline here.

Your finish line is your time times 0.9. Write and rehearse a talk that is nine-tenths the time you were given: 1 hour = 54 minutes, 10 minutes = 9, 18 minutes = 16:12 (yes, it is). Then get on stage and ignore the clock. You'll have breathing room to pace yourself, to pause, to screw up a little, to milk the audience's response. Plus your writing will be tighter and you'll stand out from the other speakers who are dancing to the rhythms of the same time limit.

Let's sum it up.

- For a high-stakes talk, it's very important to rehearse multiple times, preferably in front of people you trust.
- Work on it until it's comfortably under your allocated time limit and insist on honest feedback from your rehearsal audience.
- Your goal is to end up with a talk whose structure is second nature to you so that you can concentrate on meaning what you say.

13

OPEN AND CLOSE

What Kind of Impression Would You Like to Make?

Whether or not you memorize your talk, it's important to pay attention to how you begin and how you end it. At the beginning of your talk, you have about a minute to intrigue people with what you'll be saying. And the way you end will strongly influence how your talk is remembered.

However you deliver the rest of the talk, I strongly encourage you to script and memorize the opening minute and the closing lines. It helps with nerves, with confidence, and with impact.

FOUR WAYS TO START STRONG

Audience attention is a truly precious commodity. You always have it when you first arrive on stage. Don't fritter it away with small talk. It really, truly doesn't matter that much that you are honored to be there, or that the organizer's wife needs to be thanked. What matters is persuading the audience that they dare not switch off for a nanosecond. You want an opening that grabs people from the first moment. A surprising statement. An intriguing question. A short story. An incredible image.

There are, to be sure, occasions when you can start with a thank-you or two, especially when you're speaking at an event where there's a strong sense of community. There it may absolutely be the right thing to begin with acknowledging a couple of people. It makes *you* part of the community. But if you do this, please do it in a super-personal way, preferably with humor or genuine warmth. Bill Clinton is a master at this. He'll find a personal anecdote that makes the host feel like a million bucks, while simultaneously connecting with the rest of the guests as a result. However, even in that community setting, keep your thank-yous in check. Long, dry lists of acknowledgments are absolute attention killers in any context. And when you begin your talk proper, make sure it has a compelling opening.

Remember that every piece of content in our modern era is part of an attention war. It's fighting against thousands of other claims on people's time and energy. This is true even when you're standing on a stage in front of a seated audience. They have deadly distracters in their pockets called smartphones, which they can use to summon to their eyes a thousand outside alternatives. Once emails and texts make their claim, your talk may be doomed. And then there's that lurking demon of modern life, fatigue. All these are lethal enemies. You never want to provide someone with an excuse to zone out. You have to be a savvy general directing this war's outcome. Starting strong is one of your most important weapons.

This is especially true if your talk is being recorded for online posterity. Dozens of other enticing talks, articles, and quizzes are just one click away. If you waste the opening minute of your talk, you're going to lose a significant portion of your online audience before they ever realize there's an interesting bit. And that may make the difference between your talk going viral or dying a tragic death.

Here are four ways to stake your claim to the audience's attention.

1. Deliver a dose of drama
Your first words really do matter.

Comic Maysoon Zayid, who suffers from cerebral palsy due to a botched medical procedure at her birth, came onto the stage shaking, and began her talk like this: "I am not drunk . . . but the doctor who delivered me was." Kapow! Despite her unexpected appearance we immediately knew we were in for a treat. She owned every eyeball and every brain cell in the room.

Activist chef Jamie Oliver came to TED to accept our annual TED Prize. Here's how he opened. "Sadly, in the next 18 minutes . . . four Americans that are alive will be dead . . . through the food that they eat." I think you want to hear more.

In planning your opening, let your talk's throughline be your guide. How can you tease up the idea of your talk in the most compelling way imaginable? Ask yourself: if your talk were a movie or a novel, how would it open? That doesn't mean you have to cram something dramatic into the opening sentence; you definitely have a few moments of audience attention. But by the end of the first paragraph, something needs to land.

Zak Ebrahim came to TED2014 with an incredible story. But in his original script, he planned to open like this:

I was born in Pittsburgh, Pennsylvania, in 1983 to a loving American mother and an Egyptian father who tried their best to create a happy childhood for me. It wasn't until I was seven years old that our family dynamic started to change. My father exposed me to a side of Islam that few people, including the majority of Muslims, get to see. But, in fact, when people take the time to interact with one another, it doesn't take long to realize that, for the most part, we all want the same things out of life.

It's an OK opening . . . but it doesn't really grab you. We brainstormed with Zak, and here's his revised opening:

On November fifth, 1990, a man named El-Sayyid Nosair walked into a hotel in Manhattan and assassinated Rabbi Meir Kahane, the leader of the Jewish Defense League. Nosair was initially found not guilty of the murder, but while serving time on lesser charges, he and other men began planning attacks on a dozen New York City landmarks, including tunnels, synagogues, and the United Nations headquarters. Thankfully, those plans were foiled by an FBI informant. Sadly, the 1993 bombing of the World Trade Center was not. Nosair would eventually be convicted for his involvement in the plot. El-Sayyid Nosair is my father.

The audience was riveted. The opening worked online too, his talk quickly notching up 2 million views.

Here's the opening of the original script sent to us by sociologist Alice Goffman.

When I was a freshman in college at the University of Pennsylvania, I took a sociology class where we were supposed to go out and study the city through firsthand observation and participation. I got a job working at a cafeteria on campus, making sandwiches and salads. My boss was an African American woman in her sixties who lived in a black neighborhood not far from Penn. The next year I began tutoring her granddaughter Aisha, who was a freshman in high school.

She's just telling her story in a way that's natural to her, but by the time she got to the conference, she had a revised opening worthy of the searing passion of her talk.

On the path that American children travel to adulthood, two institutions oversee the journey. The first is the one we hear a lot about: college. College has some shortcomings. It's expensive; it leaves young people in debt. But all in all, it's a pretty good path . . .

Today I want to talk about the second institution overseeing the journey from childhood to adulthood in the United States. And that institution is prison.

That brilliant framing allowed her to talk about the tragedy of America's incarcerated in a way that demands attention: *Hey, they could have been college kids.*

Of course, it's possible to overdo the drama and actually lose people. Maybe you want to connect with the audience a little before hitting them with a dramatic thunderbolt. And you certainly don't want to oversimplify what you're going to talk about. But done right, this is a compelling way to get a talk started.

2. Ignite curiosity

If I offered you the chance to hear a talk on parasites, I'm guessing you might decline. But only if you hadn't met science writer Ed Yong. Here's how he opened his talk.

A herd of wildebeests, a shoal of fish, a flock of birds. Many animals gather in large groups that are among the most wonderful spectacles in the natural world. But why do these groups form? The common answers include things like seeking safety in numbers or hunting in packs or gathering to mate or breed, and all of these explanations, while often true, make a huge assumption about animal behavior, that the animals are in control of their own actions, that they are in charge of their bodies. And that is often not the case.

He goes on to describe how a species of shrimp huddle together only because their brains have been taken over by parasites who need the shrimp to be visible to predator flamingos in whose bellies the parasite can continue its life cycle. In less than a minute flat, your brain is doing somersaults. *Whaaat?!* Can nature really do that?? And you're crying out to know more. How? Why? What does this mean?

Igniting curiosity is the single most versatile tool at your disposal for ensuring audience engagement. If a talk's goal is to build an idea in listeners' minds, then curiosity is the fuel that powers listeners' active participation.

Neuroscientists speak of questions creating a knowledge gap that the brain fights to close. The only way the brains of the audience can do that is by having their owners listen hard to what you have to say. This is good.

How do you spark curiosity? The obvious way is to ask a question. But not just any question. A surprising question.

How do we build a better future for all? Too broad. Too much of a cliché. I'm bored already.

How did this fourteen-year-old girl, with less than $200 in her bank account, give her whole town a giant leap into the future? Now we're talking.

Sometimes a little illustration can turn a so-so question into full-on curiosity ignition. Here's how philosopher Michael Sandel began:

> Here's a question we need to rethink together: What should be the role of money and markets in our societies?

Are you interested yet? Maybe, maybe not. But here's how he continues.

> Today, there are very few things that money can't buy. If you're sentenced to a jail term in Santa Barbara, California, you should know that if you don't like the standard accommodations, you can buy a prison cell upgrade. It's true. For how much, do you think? What would you guess? Five hundred dollars? It's not the Ritz-Carlton. It's a jail! Eighty-two dollars a night.

If his opening question didn't immediately grab you, the crazy jail example reveals why the question might matter a lot after all.

In fact, curiosity-generating speakers often *don't* explicitly ask a question. At least not at first. They simply frame a topic in an unexpected way that clicks that curiosity button.

Here's V. S. Ramachandran:

> I study the human brain, the functions and structure of the human brain. And I just want you to think for a minute about what this entails. Here is this three-pound mass of jelly you can hold in the palm of your hand, and it can contemplate the vastness of interstellar space. It can contemplate the meaning of infinity and it can contemplate itself contemplating on the meaning of infinity.

Are you intrigued? I am. Likewise, astronomer Janna Levin found a way to make me intensely curious about her work.

> I want to ask you all to consider for a second the very simple fact that, by far, most of what we know about the universe comes to us from light. We can stand on the Earth and look up at the night sky and see stars with our bare eyes. The Sun burns our peripheral vision. We see light reflected off the Moon. And in the time since Galileo pointed that rudimentary telescope at the celestial bodies, the known universe has come to us through light, across vast eras in cosmic history. And with all of our modern telescopes, we've been able to collect this stunning silent movie of the universe — these series of snapshots that go all the way back to the Big Bang. And yet, the universe is not a silent movie because the universe isn't silent. I'd like to convince you that the universe has a soundtrack and that soundtrack is played on space itself, because space can wobble like a drum.

Curiosity is the magnet that pulls your audience along with you. If you can wield it effectively, you can turn even difficult subjects into winning talks.

And by "difficult subjects," I don't just mean Advanced Physics. Even harder are talks about challenging issues and causes. If you want to advance new ideas about HIV or malaria or human slavery, you have to be aware that it's hard for people to open up to these topics. They know they're going to be made to feel uncomfortable at some point. It's tempting to them to shut down ahead of time and pull out the iPhone. A great way to counter that is *to lead with curiosity.*

As mentioned earlier, Emily Oster did this in her talk about AIDS. Instead of the expected litany of horrors her audience may have been expecting, she started by asking whether the four things we all thought we knew about AIDS in Africa were actually true. She had a slide listing them. They looked right, but it was clear she was going to challenge each one. And just like that, a different part of the brain swings into action. Attention was won.

If your talk topic is challenging, curiosity is probably your most powerful engine of engagement.

3. Show a compelling slide, video, or object

Sometimes the best opening hook is a glorious, impactful, or intriguing picture or video.

Artist Alexa Meade began by showing a striking image of one of her works and speaking these words. "You may want to take a closer look. There's more to this painting than meets the eye. And yes, it's an acrylic painting of a man, but I didn't paint it on canvas. I painted it directly on top of the man." Wow.

Elora Hardy began: "When I was nine years old, my mom asked me what I would want my house to look like, and I drew this fairy mushroom." She shows a cute child's drawing. "And then she actually built it." You can hear the audience's intake of breath as she shows an image of the bamboo house her mother built. It's just the setup for a series of stunning images of Elora's own work as an architect, but look how rapidly she has engaged the audience. Two sentences in, and they're already gasping.

If you have the right material, this is clearly a great way to start a talk. Instead of saying, *"Today I plan to talk to you about my work, but first I need to give you some background . . . ,"* you can just start by saying: *"Let me show you something."*

Obviously this approach can work well for photographers, artists, architects, and designers, or others whose work is fundamentally visual. But it can also work beautifully for conceptual talks. When David Christian gave his history of the universe in 18 minutes, he began with video of an egg being scrambled. It was only after 10 seconds or so that you realized the process was happening in reverse — the egg was being *un*scrambled. Right there, right in his intriguing opening video, he revealed the throughline of his story . . . that there is a direction to time. That the story of the universe is one of growing complexity.

A gorgeous image captures attention. But the full impact often comes in revealing something surprising about it. Carl Zimmer began with a stunningly beautiful picture of a jewel wasp. But he then revealed that it made its living by turning cockroaches into zombies and laying its eggs inside their comatose bodies (another triumphant entry in that strange niche of TED Talks devoted to truly disturbing parasites).

Depending on what material you have, there are plenty of ways to ponder even more intriguing starts. *"The image you're about to see changed my life."*

"I'm going to play you a video that, at first viewing, may seem to be impossible."

"Here's my opening slide. Can you figure out what this thing is?"

"Until two and a half months ago, no living human had cast eyes on this object."

Find the one that feels right for you. Compelling, but also authentic. An opening that will boost your own confidence going into the talk.

4. Tease, but don't give it away

Occasionally, speakers try to bring too much to their opening paragraph. They essentially give away the punchline of their talk. *"Today I'm going to explain to you that the key to success as an entrepreneur is simply this: determination."* A worthy goal. But the speaker may have already lost the audience. They think they know the talk already. Even if what follows is full of nuance, logic, passion, and persuasion, they may no longer be listening.

Suppose instead the talk started this way: *"Over the next few minutes I plan to reveal what I believe is the key to success as an entrepreneur, and how anyone here can cultivate it. You'll find clues to it in the story I'm about to tell."* You'll probably give that speaker at least a few more minutes of your attention.

So instead of giving it all away up front, imagine what kind of language will seduce the audience into wanting to come along for the ride. Different audience, different language. I mentioned that, as a child, I didn't much like to be dragged out walking. My parents made a valiant effort at audience empathy . . . but failed. They'd say, *"Let's go for a hike. We'll get to see a beautiful view of the valley."* And the unfit little six-year-old that was me, who frankly didn't care at all about views, would whine all the way there and back. Later, they got wise and went for a more cleverly crafted pitch. *"We've got a treat for you. We're going somewhere special where you can launch a paper airplane into five miles of empty space."* As a fan of anything that flew, I was out the door before they were. It was the same walk.

It's OK to save the big revelations for the middle or end of your talk. In the opening sentences your sole goal is to give your audience a reason to step away from their comfort zone and accompany you on an amazing journey of discovery.

As J. J. Abrams pointed out in his TED Talk on the power of mystery, the movie *Jaws* owes a lot of its impact to the fact that director Steven Spielberg hid the shark for the first half of the movie. You knew it was coming, for sure. But its invisibility helped keep you on the edge of your seat.

As you plan your talk, there's no harm in channeling your inner Spielberg. Edith Widder did just that, albeit with help from a different sea creature. When she gave a talk on her team's discovery of the giant squid, she of course wanted a powerful opening. Did she show the amazing footage of the squid? Oh no. Instead, her opening slide was a dramatic artist's image of the kraken, the squidlike sea monster of Norwegian legend. That allowed her to set up the story she was going to tell as rooted deep in mythology. The moment when the giant squid appears is a hundred times more dramatic for being held back.

The technique works for astonishing creatures, and it also works for astonishing breakthroughs. Stanford professor Fei-Fei Li came to TED in 2015 to present her remarkable work, showing how machine learning has enabled computers to visually identify the contents of photographs. But she didn't start with a demo. She started with a video of a three-year-old child looking at pictures and identifying their contents. "That's a cat sitting in a bed." "The boy is petting the elephant." She then helped us understand how amazing the skill being demonstrated by the child was, and how consequential it would be if we could train computers to develop similar capabilities. It was a beautiful setup to describe her work. The jaw-dropping demos of artificial intelligence came later, and we were hooked all the way.

If you decide to tease a little, please note that it's still very important to indicate where you're going and why. You don't have to show the shark, but we do need to know it's coming. Every talk needs mapping—*a sense of where you're going, where you are, and where you've been.* If your listeners don't know where they are in the structure of the talk, they will quickly get lost.

In crafting your own opening, you can draw inspiration from any or all of the above. You can also build in some of the techniques discussed earlier: tell a story, maybe, or get people laughing. The key is simply to find a good fit for you and for what you're talking about. Test it on friends. If it feels contrived or overly dramatic, change it. Just bear in mind that your goal is to persuade someone, in only a few moments, that your talk is going to be a worthy investment of their attention.

When I was in the magazine business, I urged our editors and designers to think of magazine covers as having to compete in a two-stage war for attention. First, the half-second war: as someone's eyes scanned across a newsstand, was there something attention-grabbing on the cover that would make her stop for a moment? Next, the 5-second war: once she'd stopped to look, would she read something compelling enough on the cover to make her pick up the magazine?

You can think of a talk opening the same way, except with different timings. First there is the 10-second war: can you do something in your first moments on stage to ensure people's eager attention while you set up your talk topic? Second is the 1-minute war: can you then use that first minute to ensure that they're committed to coming on the full talk journey with you?

The four techniques above offer excellent options for winning both stages of that war, thereby giving your talk its best shot. You may want to combine two or more of them in your opening, though you certainly shouldn't try to use all of them. Pick the ones that feel right to you. And then you, and your fully engaged audience, will be on your way together.

SEVEN WAYS TO END WITH POWER

If you've held people's attention through the talk, don't ruin it with a flat ending. As Danny Kahneman explained so powerfully in both his book *Thinking, Fast and Slow* and in his TED Talk, how people remember an event may be very different from how they experienced it, and when it comes to remembering, your final experience is really important. In short, if the ending isn't memorable, the talk itself may not be.

Here's how *not* to end:

- "Well, that's my time gone, so I'll wrap up there." *(You mean, you had a lot more to say but can't tell us because of bad planning?)*
- "Finally, I just want to thank my awesome team, who are pictured here: David, Joanna, Gavin, Samantha, Lee, Abdul, and Hezekiah. Also, my university, and my sponsors." *(Lovely, but do you care about them more than your idea, and more than us, your audience?!)*
- "So, given the importance of this issue, I hope we can start a new conversation about it together." *(A conversation?! Isn't that a little lame? What should be the outcome of that conversation?)*
- "The future is full of challenges and opportunities. Everyone here has it in their heart to make a difference. Let's dream together. Let's be the change we want to see in the world." *(Beautiful sentiment, but the clichés really don't help anyone.)*
- "I'll close with this video which summarizes my points." *(No! Never end with a video. End with you!)*
- "So that concludes my argument, now are there any questions?" *(Or, how to preempt your own applause.)*

- "I'm sorry I haven't had time to discuss some of the major issues here, but hopefully this has at least given you a flavor of the topic." (*Don't apologize! Plan more carefully! Your job was to give the best talk you could in the time available.*)
- "In closing, I should just point out that my organization could probably solve this problem if we were adequately funded. You have it in your power to change the world with us." (*Ah, so this was a fundraising pitch all along?*)
- "Thanks for being such an amazing audience. I have loved every moment, standing here, talking to you. I'll carry this experience with me for a long, long time. You've been so patient, and I know that you'll take what you've heard today and do something wonderful with it." (*"Thank you" would have been just fine.*)

It's amazing how many talks simply fizzle out. And how many more go through a series of false endings, as if the speaker can't bear to leave the stage. Unless you plan your ending carefully, you may well find yourself adding paragraph after paragraph. *Finally, the key point, as I said . . . So, in conclusion . . . And just to emphasize again, the reason this matters . . . And of course it's important to still bear in mind . . . Oh, and one last thing . . .* It's exhausting. And it will damage the talk's impact.

Here are seven better ways to end:

Camera pull-back

You've spent the talk explaining a particular piece of work. At the end, why not show us the bigger picture, a broader set of possibilities implied by your work?

David Eagleman showed that the human brain could be thought of as a pattern recognizer, and that if you were to connect new electrical data to a brain, it could come to interpret that data as if coming from a brand-new sense organ, so that you could intuitively sense brand-new aspects of the world in real time. He ended by hinting at the limitless possibilities this brought with it.

> Just imagine an astronaut being able to feel the overall health of the International Space Station, or, for that matter, having you feel the invisible states of your own health, like your blood sugar and the state of your microbiome, or having 360-degree vision or seeing in infrared or ultraviolet. So the key is this: As we move into the future, we're going to increasingly be able to choose our own peripheral devices. We no longer have to wait for Mother Nature's sensory gifts on her timescales, but instead, like any good parent, she's given us the tools that we need to go out and define our own trajectory. So the question now is, how do you want to go out and experience your universe?

Call to action

If you've given your audience a powerful idea, why not end by nudging them to act on it?

Harvard Business School professor Amy Cuddy concluded her talk on power posing by inviting people to try it in their own lives, and to pass it on to others.

> Give it away. Share it with people, because the people who can use it the most are the ones with no resources and no technology and no status and no power. Give it to them because they can do it in private. They need their bodies, privacy, and 2 minutes, and it can significantly change the outcomes of their life.

Perhaps that confident call contributed to the talk's extraordinary viral success.

In his talk on public shaming, author Jon Ronson's final call to action was admirably succinct.

The great thing about social media was how it gave a voice to voiceless people, but we're now creating a surveillance society, where the smartest way to survive is to go back to being voiceless. Let's not do that.

Personal commitment

It's one thing to call on the audience to act, but sometimes speakers score by making a giant commitment of their own. The most dramatic example of this at TED was when Bill Stone spoke of the possibilities of humans returning to the moon, and his conviction that an expedition could create a massive new industry and open up space exploration for a new generation. Then he said this:

> I would like to close here by putting a stake in the sand at TED.
> I intend to lead that expedition.

A personal commitment like that can be incredibly compelling. Remember the Elon Musk example from chapter 1? *"For my part, I will never give up and I mean never."* That was the key to reenergizing his SpaceX team.

In 2011, the swimmer Diana Nyad gave a TED Talk in which she described how she had tried to do what no one had ever achieved, to swim from Cuba to Florida. She had tried on three occasions, sometimes persisting for 50 hours of constant swimming, braving dangerous currents and near-lethal jellyfish stings, but ultimately failing. At the end of her talk she electrified the audience by saying this:

> That ocean's still there. This hope is still alive. And I don't want to be the crazy woman who does it for years and years and years, and tries and fails and tries and fails and tries and fails . . .

I can swim from Cuba to Florida, and I will swim from Cuba to Florida.

And sure enough, two years later she returned to the TED stage to describe how, at age sixty-four, she had finally done it.

As with everything, making a major commitment requires judgment. Done wrong, it could lead to awkwardness in the moment, and a loss of credibility later. But if you're passionate about turning an idea into action, it may well be worth stepping up to.

Values and vision

Can you turn what you've discussed into an inspiring or hopeful vision of what might be? Many speakers try. The late Rita Pierson, who gave a beautiful talk on how teachers need to build real relationships with their kids, ended with this:

> Teaching and learning should bring joy. How powerful would our world be if we had kids who were not afraid to take risks, who were not afraid to think, and who had a champion? Every child deserves a champion, an adult who will never give up on them, who understands the power of connection, and insists that they become the best that they can possibly be. Is this job tough? You betcha. Oh God, you betcha. But it is not impossible. We can do this. We're educators. We're born to make a difference. Thank you so much.

Rita passed away a couple of months after giving this talk, but her call continues to resonate. Teacher Kitty Boitnott wrote a moving tribute: "I did not know her and I did not know of her until today, but today, through her talk, she touched my life and reminded me why I was a teacher for over three decades."

Satisfying encapsulation

Sometimes speakers find a way to neatly reframe the case they've been making. Therapist Esther Perel called for a new, more honest approach to infidelity that included the possibility of forgiveness. She ended like this:

> I look at affairs from a dual perspective: hurt and betrayal on one side, growth and self-discovery on the other — what it did to you, and what it meant for me. And so when a couple comes to me in the aftermath of an affair that has been revealed, I will often tell them this: Today in the West, most of us are going to have two or three relationships or marriages, and some of us are going to do it with the same person. Your first marriage is over. Would you like to create a second one together?

And Amanda Palmer, who has challenged the music industry to rethink its business model, ended this way:

> I think people have been obsessed with the wrong question, which is, "How do we make people pay for music?" What if we started asking, "How do we let people pay for music?"

In both cases, a surprising question carried with it a pleasing moment of insight and closure, and prompted a long standing ovation.

Narrative symmetry

A talk built carefully on a throughline can deliver a pleasing conclusion by linking back to its opening. Steven Johnson began his talk on where ideas come from by revealing the significance of coffeehouses in industrial Britain. They were places where intellectuals gathered to spark off each other. Toward the end he told the powerful story of how GPS was invented, illustrating all his points on how ideas emerge. And then, brilliantly, he threw in the fact that GPS was probably used by everyone in the audience that week to do things like . . . find their nearest coffeehouse. You can hear in the audience a little gasp of appreciation and applause at the satisfying way the narrative has come full circle.

Lyrical inspiration

Sometimes, if the talk has opened people up, it's possible to end with poetic language that taps deep into matters of the heart. This should not be tried lightly. But when it works, it's quite beautiful. Here's how Brené Brown ended her talk on vulnerability.

> This is what I have found: to let ourselves be seen, deeply seen, vulnerably seen; to love with our whole hearts, even though there's no guarantee . . . to practice gratitude and joy in those moments of terror, when we're wondering, *Can I love you this much? Can I believe in this passionately? Can I be this fierce about this?* just to be able to stop . . . and say, "I'm just so grateful, because to feel this vulnerable means I'm alive." And the last, which I think is probably the most important, is to believe that we're enough. Because when we work from a place, I believe, that says, I'm enough, then we stop screaming and start listening, we're kinder and gentler to the people around us, and we're kinder and gentler to ourselves. That's all I have. Thank you.

And human-rights lawyer Bryan Stevenson closed his blockbuster talk on the injustices of the US prison system with this:

> I've come to TED because I believe that many of you understand that the moral arc of the universe is long, but it bends toward justice. That we cannot be fully evolved human beings until we care about human rights and basic dignity. That all of our survival is tied to the survival of everyone. That our visions of tech-

nology and design and entertainment and creativity have to be married with visions of humanity, compassion, and justice. And more than anything, for those of you who share that, I've simply come to tell you to keep your eyes on the prize, hold on.

I repeat, you cannot do this lightly. It only works when the rest of the talk has already prepared the groundwork, and when it's clear the speaker has earned the right to evoke such sentiment. But in the right hands and at the right moment, these closings can be transcendent.

Whichever way you end, make sure it's planned. An elegant closing paragraph, followed by a simple "thank you," offers the best shot at a satisfying end to your efforts. It's worth figuring out.

On Stage

14
WARDROBE
What Should I Wear?

Many speakers worry about the clothes they should wear to make the best impression. And I'm probably the last person they should turn to for advice. I'm the guy who showed up on stage one year with my beautiful, bright yellow sleeveless sweater vest over a hip-as-hell black T-shirt and black trousers, thinking I looked terrific, while the audience simply wondered, *Why did that man dress as a bumblebee?*

I therefore have handed over this section to TED's content director, Kelly Stoetzel, who has both fabulous style and a magnificent ability to put speakers at their ease. Here's her advice.

Kelly Stoetzel writes:

The last thing you need is wardrobe stress in the hours leading up to your talk, and selecting an outfit is one thing you can check off your to-do list early.

In most settings all that matters is that you wear something you feel great in. At TED, we like reasonably casual clothes, giving the sense that we're all on a retreat together. Other places may expect a suit and tie. You probably don't want the audience's first unconscious thought about you to be any of the following: *stodgy, slovenly, tasteless, boring,* or *trying too hard.* But if you avoid those potential traps, wearing something that makes you feel good will help you project relaxed confidence. And audiences will respond to that. Believe it or not, your clothing can earn you an audience connection before you've even spoken a word.

As you think about what you'll wear, there are a few questions worth asking, such as, *Is there a dress code? How is the audience likely to be dressed?* You'll probably want to dress somewhat like they do, but a little bit smarter.

Will you be filmed? If so, avoid wearing brilliant white (it can blow out the shot) or jet black (you might look like a floating head), or anything with a small or tight pattern (it can cause a strange, shimmery, moiré effect on camera).

Will you be using an over-the-ear microphone? There are some risks here: Several times a speaker had just started speaking when strange, loud, clanking noises erupted from nowhere. They're caused by earrings banging into the microphone attachment. Avoid dangling earrings! Also, men's beard stubble can cause scratching sounds.

If you're choosing accessories, avoid jangly bracelets or anything flashy that might cause a reflection. Scarves can be a good way to bring in a pop of color if you've chosen to wear something neutral.

You'll likely be wearing the mike's battery pack on your belt, and you'll probably feel most secure if you have a firm belt or defined waistline where you can attach the pack.

What will the stage look like? Consider wearing something bright that sets you apart from the background. Think about dressing for the people sitting in the back row. TEDWomen speaker Linda Cliatt-Wayman wore a beautiful bright-pink dress that ensured she didn't blend in, and all eyes were on her from the moment she took the stage until her final applause.

The audience loves bold, vibrant colors, and so does the camera.

Fitted clothing tends to look better on stage than outfits that are loose and baggy. Look for something with a nice silhouette, and make sure it's the right size — not too slack, not too tight.

While it's good to consider these guidelines, personal expressions of style can trump them all. A couple of weeks before TED2015, we sent out a note to speakers with a few final reminders, including a recommendation that men steer clear of ties. Radio host Roman Mars replied with, "Why no ties? Ties are great." We told him that if ties were his special thing, then he should simply ignore our suggestion. He wore one, he felt great, looked great, and fit right in. Book designer Chip Kidd has also delightfully broken the TED no-tie rule with his strong, wonderful sense of style.

If you're still unsure what to wear, book a shopping date with a friend whose taste you trust. Sometimes the way you see yourself in the mirror isn't exactly the same way others see you. I almost always do this myself, and I've regretted it the times I haven't. Another opinion can be invaluable.

Before you take the stage, be sure your clothes are neatly pressed. Wrinkled clothes are the single easiest way to telegraph that you didn't try very hard. If you're speaking late in the day, it may even be worth bringing your clothes on a hanger and changing into them closer to the time of your presentation. An important lesson I've learned the hard way: If you plan to use a hotel iron, press your clothes the night before and test the iron on a towel first. Those irons often aren't in the best shape, and they can be leaky or even dirty. (The TED Fellows team brings a small, packable, personal steamer with them to help wrinkled speakers!)

It's worth rehearsing your talk in the outfit you plan to wear. I remember a speaker whose clothing shifted early in her talk so that both bra straps fell off her shoulders and were hanging down on her arms through almost the entire talk. Our editors were able to work some magic so you can't notice this mishap in the video, but it could have been avoided completely with a dress rehearsal and a couple of safety pins.

Once again, the most important thing is just to wear something that boosts your confidence. This is something you can control in advance. And it will give you one less thing to worry about and one more thing working in your favor.

And back to Chris:

Thank you, Kelly. People, take note!

And when all's said and done, don't overthink this part. Your passion and your ideas matter a lot more than how you look.

When Professor Barry Schwartz showed up at the TED stage in Oxford for his talk on the paradox of choice, it was a hot summer's day, and he was wearing a T-shirt and shorts. He tells me if he'd known we were going to video him and put him online, he might have chosen something else. But it didn't stop his talk notching up 7 million views.

Amanda Palmer says her sole regret of her talk prep was choosing a gray shirt that turned black with underarm perspiration. But the audience thought it was just part of her break-the-rules approach to life, and the talk was a massive hit both live and online.

So, in summary:

1. Do what Kelly says.
2. Make an early commitment to an outfit you'll feel great in.
3. Focus on your ideas, not your clothes!

15
MENTAL PREP
How Do I Control My Nerves?

Fear triggers our ancient fight-or-flight response. Your body is coiled up chemically, ready to strike or flee. This is measurable physically by a huge rise in adrenaline coursing through your bloodstream.

Adrenaline's great for powering a sprint to safety across the savannah, and it can certainly bring energy and excitement to your stage presence. But too much of it is a bad thing. It can dry up your mouth and tighten your throat. Its job is to turbo-charge your muscles, and if your muscles are not being used, the adrenaline rush may start them twitching, hence the shaking associated with extreme cases of nerves.

Some coaches advise medication in such cases, typically beta-blockers, but the downside is that they can deaden your tone. There are plenty of other counterstrategies to turn all that adrenaline to your advantage.

Let's return to Monica Lewinsky. In chapter 1 she described the intensity of her nervousness in approaching her TED Talk. If she could overcome her nerves, I'm guessing you can too. In her own words, here's how she did it:

> In some forms of meditation, the guidance is to return to the breath or your mantra when your mind wanders or "monkey mind" sets in. I did that with my anxiety. I tried my best to return to the purpose of my speech as often as possible. One of

my two mantras was *THIS MATTERS*. (In fact, I had scrawled it across the top of page one of my speech that was on stage with me.) The other mantra that worked well for me was *I'VE GOT THIS*.

If you are going to be standing on a stage, addressing an audience, it means someone, somewhere decided you had something of import to impart to others. I spent time articulating to myself how I hoped my speech might help others who were suffering. I clung to the meaning and purpose of my speech as a life raft.

I had tools that worked for me. I pulled out all the stops in terms of support and having my tanks as full as possible for the day of the speech and leading up to it. I have spent a lot of time in the last seventeen years learning to manage my anxiety and past trauma. The morning of the speech, in no particular order, I used bioresonance sound work, breathing exercises, a therapy called Emotional Freedom Technique (commonly known as "tapping," I did this backstage moments before going on), chanted, did various warm-up exercises with my public-speaking coach, went for a walk to move the adrenaline in my body, made sure I laughed at least once, grounding visualization, and lastly, I power posed (lucky me, with the inimitable Amy Cuddy).

There was more than one moment where I doubted my ability to see the speech through. The night before the speech content rehearsal, three weeks before the conference, I broke down in tears, exasperated that the content was just not gelling. I planned to bow out after the rehearsal but I was shocked by the positive reception. I kept waiting for the *However* . . . and *But*. They never came.

I sat with the response for a long time after, still unsure, but I ultimately concluded, if people who knew what they were doing when it came to TED Talks thought the speech was compelling enough, I should stick with it; I was simply too close to it.

Throughout the process, when faced with self-doubt, I focused as much as I could on the message to deliver, instead of the messenger. Whenever I felt nervous or unsure, I had to simply steel myself and try to self-reason that all I could do was my best . . . and that if I could reach one person with my message and help just one person feel less alone in their experience of shame and online humiliation, it would be worth it.

The experience proved to be life changing for me on many levels.

That's as exhaustive a set of nervousness-controlling tools as you'll ever see. Should you try to adopt every one of Monica's techniques? No. Everyone's different. But the fact that she was able to turn crippling fear into a calm, confident, engaging stage presence should encourage anyone that it can be done.

Here's what I recommend:

Use your fear as motivation. That's what it's there for. It will make it easier for you to truly commit to practicing your talk as many times as it takes. In doing that, your confidence will rise, your fear will ebb, and your talk will be better than it otherwise would have been.

Let your body help you! There's a series of important things you can do before going on stage that really help circumvent the adrenaline rush. The single most important one is to *breathe*. Breathe deeply, meditation style. The oxygen infusion brings calm with it. You can do this even if you're seated in the audience, waiting to be called up. Just take a deep breath right into your stomach, and let it out slowly. Repeat three times more. If you're offstage and you're feeling tension surging through your body, it's worth trying more vigorous physical exercise.

At TED2014, I was super-stressed about the prospect of interviewing Richard Ledgett of the NSA about the Edward Snowden controversy. Ten minutes before the session, I escaped to a backstage corridor and started doing pushups. And I couldn't stop. I ended up doing 30 percent more than I thought was the most I was capable of. It was all adrenaline, and by burning it that way, calm and confidence returned.

Drink water. The worst aspect of nerves is when the adrenaline sucks the water from your mouth and you struggle to speak. Controlling the adrenaline, as above, is the best antidote, but it's also good to make sure you're fully hydrated. Five minutes before you go on, try to drink a third of a bottle of water. It'll help stop your mouth from getting dry. (But don't do this too early. Salman Khan did, and then had to rush to the men's room just before his introduction. He was back in the nick of time.)

Avoid an empty stomach. When you're nervous, eating may be the last thing you want to do, but an empty stomach can exacerbate anxiety. Get some healthy food into your body an hour or so before you're on, and/or have a protein bar handy.

Remember the power of vulnerability. Audiences embrace speakers who are nervous, especially if the speaker can find a way to acknowledge it. If you flub or stutter a little in your opening remarks, it's fine to say, "Ooops, sorry, a little nervous here." Or "As you can see, I don't do a lot of public speaking. But this one mattered too much to turn down." Your listeners will begin rooting for you even more.

At a packed Sydney Opera House, singer/songwriter Megan Washington confessed to the TEDx audience that she had battled all her life with the stutter they could hear. Her honesty and initial awkwardness made the song she flawlessly performed all the more glorious.

Find "friends" in the audience. Early on in the talk, look out for faces that seem sympathetic. If you can find three or four in different parts of the audience, give the talk to them, moving your gaze from one to the next in turn. Everyone in the audience will see you connecting, and the encouragement you get from those faces will bring you calm and confidence. Maybe you even ensure that some of your actual friends are seated around the auditorium. Speak to *them*. (As an aside, speaking to friends will help you find the right tone of voice, too.)

Have a backup plan. If you're worried about things going wrong, plan a few backup moves. You fear you might forget what you were going to say? Have notes or a script within reach. (Roz Savage had hers tucked inside her shirt. No one minded at all when she lost her way a couple of times and referred to them.) Scared the technology may go wrong and you'll have to vamp? Well, first of all, that's the organizer's problem, not yours, but no harm in having a little story to tell if you need to fill in, all the better if it's personal. "While they sort that out, let me share with you a conversation I just had with a taxi driver . . ." or "Oh, this is great. Now I have a chance to mention to you something I had to cut from the talk for time reasons . . ." Or "Great, we have a couple of extra minutes. So let *me* ask a question of *you*. Who here has ever . . ."

Focus on what you're talking about. Monica's suggestion to write THIS MATTERS on your notes is wonderful. This is the single biggest piece of advice I can give you. It's not about you, it's about the idea you're passionate about. Your job is to be there in service of that idea, to offer it as a gift. If you can hold that in mind as you walk onto the stage, you'll find it liberating.

Singer Joe Kowan was paralyzed by nerves to the point that it prevented him from doing what he most loved: singing to people. So he took it on, one step at a time, forcing himself to perform in small venues even when he could hear the nervous squeak in his voice, and eventually writing a stage fright song that he'd wheel out in performances if need be. Audiences loved it, and he came to embrace his nerves as friends. He has a delightful talk (and song) explaining how he did it.

At a conference in Toronto fifteen years ago, I watched as novelist Barbara Gowdy froze on stage. She simply stood there quaking. She couldn't speak. She had thought she was going to be interviewed but at the last minute was told she had to speak. The fear was oozing out of every pore in her body. But the most amazing thing happened. The audience began applauding her and cheering. She started hesitantly, stopped. More applause. And then she began sharing the most eloquent, intimate insights into her thinking and process. It was the most memorable talk of that conference. If she'd just come on confidently and started speaking we wouldn't have listened as closely, or cared as intensely.

Nerves are not a curse. They can be turned to great effect. Make friends with your nervousness, pluck up your courage — and go!

16
SETUP
Lectern, Confidence Monitor, Note Cards, or (Gulp) Nothing?

The physical setup of your talk really matters. Compare setup A: a speaker standing on a podium behind a big, bulky lectern, reading from a script to a somewhat distant audience, with setup B: a speaker standing unprotected on a small stage surrounded on three sides by an audience.

Both are called public speaking, but they're actually very different activities. Setup B can seem terrifying. You stand there, vulnerable, with no laptop, no script, your whole body visible, nowhere to hide, painfully aware of all the eyes staring at you from not very far away.

Setup A has evolved over the years to accommodate every speaker need. Before electricity, a speaker might have had a small lectern on which to place some notes. But over the twentieth century, lecterns (or podiums) got bigger and bigger to accommodate a light for the script, buttons to advance slides, and, more recently, a laptop. There was even a theory that by blocking out most of the speaker's body so you could only see her face, you were boosting her authority, perhaps by unconscious association with a preacher in a pulpit. Whether deliberate or unintentional, the effect of larger lecterns has been to create a huge visual barrier between speaker and audience.

From a speaker's point of view, this can be very comfortable. What's not to like? All you need for your talk is right there at your fingertips. And you feel personally secure. The fact that you forgot to shine your shoes or that your shirt is a little wrinkled just doesn't matter. No one can see that. Do you have awkward body language or bad posture? No problem. The lectern hides that too. Pretty much all that's visible is your face. Phew! And hurrah!

But from the audience's point of view, there's a big loss here. We spent a whole chapter talking about the importance of making a connection between audience and speaker. And a significant part of that is driven by the speaker's willingness to be vulnerable. It's an unspoken but powerful interaction. If a speaker lets down his guard, so does the audience. If a speaker stays distant and safe, the audience will too.

TED's cofounder, Richard Saul Wurman, was adamant on this point. No podiums! No lecterns! No reading of speeches! He disliked anything that turned the relationship between audience and speaker into something formal. (That included the wearing of ties, which he banned outright. When one speaker, Nicholas Negroponte, demurred and showed up in a suit and tie, Richard strode on stage with a pair of scissors and cut off the tie!)

That stance is one of the reasons why TED conferences felt different from what people were used to. Speakers were *forced* to be vulnerable. And audiences responded.

If you can get comfortable with it, a talk given in front of an audience with no lectern in the way is the best approach. The vast majority of TED Talks are like this, and we encourage everyone to give it a try. But there are tradeoffs, and in today's TED, we've concluded that there are multiple ways to give a talk, both for variety's sake, and to meet the needs of a given speaker. It's good for speakers to push the edge of their comfort zone. But as I described earlier, you can also go too far. I learned from Daniel Kahneman and others that letting someone speak in a setup that makes him feel confident and allows him to most naturally find the words he needs matters even more than maximizing vulnerability.

So the purpose of this chapter is to help you understand the full set of tradeoffs and then find the speaking mode that is best for you.

The key first question: in order to give your talk effectively, how many notes will you need to refer to? If you have it memorized completely, or you can deliver it from a short handwritten set of bullet points, the choice is simple. Go out on stage and give the talk direct, human to humans. No lectern, nothing in the way, just you, a single hand-held note card, and the audience. In many ways this is the gold standard to aim for. It's your best chance at building a powerful connection with your listeners, building on your perceived vulnerability.

But not everyone can get comfortable with this approach, and perhaps not every talk justifies the time it takes to do well in this situation.

So if you think you need a lot more notes, or even a full script, what then? Here's a list of possibilities that offer progressively more support. But some are much better than others.

COMFORT BACKUP

In this mode, before going on stage, you place a full set of notes or even a script on a table or lectern at the side or back of the stage, along with a bottle of water. You then seek to deliver the talk from the front of the stage as above, knowing that if you get stuck, you can move to your notes, take a sip of water, and continue. From an audience point of view, this is completely natural and nonproblematic. By having the notes at a distance from you, you'll avoid the temptation of looking down at every instance, and chances are good that you will get through the talk without even having to use them. But it takes away a lot of pressure just to know they're there.

SLIDES AS GUIDES

Many speakers use their slides as memory nudges. We discussed this briefly earlier in the book. What you mustn't do, of course, is to use PowerPoint as a full outline of your talk and deliver a series of text-crammed slides. That's awful. But if you have elegant images to accompany each key step of your talk, this approach can work very well, provided that you've thought about each transition. The images act as terrific memory nudges, though you may still need to carry a card with additional notes.

HAND-HELD NOTE CARDS

Maybe you have too much to fit on a single card. You want to remind yourself what the transition is to each slide, the key examples that go under each main bullet point, or the exact phrasing of your closing. In that case, the best bet may be to use a set of hand-held 5 x 8 inch cards, which you simply page through one by one. It's best to have them on a ring clip, in case you drop them and they get out of sequence. These cards are unobtrusive, but they allow you to easily check where you are in your talk. The only downside is if you rarely need to refer to them, and then have to page through five or six to catch up with your next point.

An alternative is a clipboard or full-size sheets of paper. They require fewer page turns, but overall seem more intrusive. Cards are probably better, and if your talk relies a lot on visuals, a good approach is one card per slide that includes the transition text to the following slide.

All this being said, it's still important to know your talk pretty well so you're not constantly looking down.

Many TED speakers use note cards. You may not see them onscreen, but that's partly because our editors have done a good job disguising them, and partly because most speakers use them only as occasional support. The power of this approach is that it frees you to walk the stage unencumbered, while still carrying with you all you need in terms of keeping the talk on track.

SMARTPHONE OR TABLET

Some speakers have taken to using smart devices as a high-tech replacement for note cards. Instead of multiple cards, they figure they can simply scroll through their talk. This approach can certainly grant someone freedom from the lectern. But I'm not crazy about it. For one thing, when someone's looking at a screen, we unconsciously associate that with their being disconnected from us. All that texting is to blame.

In addition, there are many things that can slow this down. A single accidental touch on the screen can take you away from your script, and it may take *a lot* of scrolling and peering to find your place. Perhaps someone will come up with the perfect app to fix this, but so far, as used in real-world conditions, this solution seems slower and clumsier than old-fashioned note cards. It's fine to have your script on an iPad and to use it as a comfort backup, but I don't recommend using a smart device for notes you regularly refer to.

CONFIDENCE MONITORS

Many higher-end speaking venues will have a couple of "confidence" monitors in your field of vision, either angled up from the floor of the stage or perhaps at the back of the room above the audience. The main purpose of these is to allow you to see that your slide has advanced without your having to constantly turn around. But they can also be used to display (for your eyes only) notes you've added to a slide, and/or the next slide due up so that you can be ready. PowerPoint and Keynote both support this feature with Presenter View. There are obvious advantages here. If you've structured your talk to have one slide per topic, you can use confidence monitors to keep yourself comfortably on track. But there are also significant traps you can fall into.

Sometimes speakers look at the wrong monitor, confuse the *next* and *current* slide screens, and panic that the wrong slide is showing. But much worse is the tendency to become too dependent on the notes on these screens and to be constantly referring to them. This is actually more off-putting than a speaker looking down at notes. Unless the confidence monitors have been placed right in the middle of the audience, you can clearly see when a speaker is looking at the screens. Either their eyes are constantly dropping to the stage floor, or they're lifting above the heads of the audience. It can become deeply off-putting, the very opposite of the sought-after eye contact that builds recognition.

Besides, there's something familiar and comfortable about a speaker occasionally referring to notes. The notes are right there and everyone can see what he's doing. It's no problem. But when his eyes move to a confidence monitor, it can quickly become distancing. You may not notice it early in a talk, but as it continues to happen, you as an audience member start to feel a little awkward. It's a bit like the Uncanny Valley I referred to earlier. Things are almost right, but not quite. And the gap feels weird.

This can get really bad when a speaker tries to read an entire speech from confidence monitors. The first 2 minutes of the talk are great, but then it starts to dawn on people that they're being read to, and somehow the life is then sucked from the talk. We had a distressing instance of this at TED a decade ago, when a sports celebrity came to give a talk and persuaded us he needed the full text of the speech on screens at the back of the room. The words he spoke were perfectly fine. But you could track his eyes reading, 3 feet above everyone's heads, and it killed the talk's impact stone dead.

The only speaker I've ever seen read effectively off confidence monitors is the singer Bono. He's a natural performer, and he managed to read out of the edge of his field of vision while maintaining lots of eye contact with the audience, a natural tone of voice, and pleasant injections of humor. But even then, people who noticed that the words of the speech, including the jokes, were right there on the monitors at the back of the hall were disappointed. They wanted Bono's mind live there with them. A written speech could have been emailed to them.

Our strong recommendation for use of confidence monitors is: use them only to show your slides, the same slides the audience is seeing. If you must add notes, use as few as possible, and with just two- or three-word bullet points. And then practice giving the talk with the absolute minimum number of glances at those monitors. No reading! That's the only way to stay warmly connected to the audience.

TELEPROMPTER/AUTOCUE

If confidence monitors are dangerous, a teleprompter is even more so. On the face of it, it's a brilliant invention. It places the words on a glass screen invisible to the audience but right in the speaker's line of sight. So a speaker can read a speech while also maintaining constant eye contact with the audience.

But its ingenuity is also its Achilles' heel. If you use one of these you're in danger of communicating to the audience, *I'm pretending to look at you, but actually I'm reading.* And the mixed signals from that can be damaging.

You might object — this can't be right. President Obama, one of the finest speakers of our era, regularly uses a teleprompter. Indeed. And it has a divisive effect on audiences. Those disposed to trust and like him ignore it and embrace the talk in full as his authentic way of speaking to them. But his political opponents have gleefully used the teleprompter against him, mocking him for not being able to speak openly to live audiences. As a result, media strategist Fred Davis believes the teleprompter has been ruined for all politicians. He told the *Washington Post*, "It's a negative because it's a sign of inauthenticity. It's a sign that you can't speak on your own two feet. It's a sign that you have handlers behind you telling you what to say."

At TED, we're reluctant to make hard and fast rules these days, but we always discourage the use of teleprompters on the main stage. Today's audiences would rather have a speaker do his best job with memory, notes, and in-the-moment thinking than do a "perfect" job that mixes reading with fake eye contact.

So what do you do if you need a full script of your talk but you can't read it off confidence monitors or a teleprompter for fear of seeming inauthentic? Here's our suggestion.

UNOBTRUSIVE LECTERN

If you must refer to a full script, lengthy notes, a laptop, or a tablet, don't fake it. Just go back to putting them on a lectern. But at least see if the event organizer can provide a cool, modern, unobtrusive lectern, one that is transparent or has a thin stem as opposed to a heavy wooden one that screens out your entire body. Then commit to knowing the talk really well, so that you can spend lots of time looking out at the audience instead of down at the lectern.

For Monica Lewinsky's talk, this proved the perfect solution.

For her, the stakes were too great to risk memorizing the entire thing. In rehearsal she tried referring to her notes from confidence monitors, but we really didn't think that approach was working. She kept looking out above the audience's heads, and it broke their connection with her. Happily, Monica came up with something we'd never tried at TED before, but which worked perfectly: she propped her notes on a music stand. If you watch her talk, you'll see that it doesn't remove her from the audience one bit. In fact she rarely looks down at it. But it gave her all the confidence she needed to truly shine.

Why does this work better than confidence monitors or a teleprompter? Because there's no ambiguity about what's happening. It's honest and familiar. The audience can enjoy the fact that you're clearly making an effort *not* to read the speech, looking around, making eye contact, smiling, and being natural. And if this makes you more comfortable and confident, people will hear that in your voice and will relax with you.

So, those are your main choices. You can, of course, always invent something unique to you. Clifford Stoll had five bullet points for his talk and wrote one on each finger, and his thumb. Every time he changed topic, the camera would zoom in to a close-up of his hand, and we'd get his view of what was next. It was quirky and endearing.

What matters is that you find the talk mode that works for you, commit to it early, and practice it as best you can, using the exact same props that you'll be using on stage. (That, by the way, is another ding against too much dependency on confidence monitors. You can never be 100 percent sure that the onstage setup is the same as what you've rehearsed with.)

In short, it's OK to be vulnerable. It's also OK to find your place of comfort and confidence. And it's essential to be authentic.

17

VOICE AND PRESENCE

Give Your Words the Life
They Deserve

Here's a radical question: Why bother to give a talk?

Why not instead simply email the text to every potential member of the audience?

An 18-minute talk contains maybe 2,500 words. Many people can read 2,500 words in less than 9 minutes and retain good comprehension. So why not do that instead? Save the auditorium cost. Save everyone's travel. Save the chance that you might flub your lines and look foolish. And get your talk across in less than half the time it takes to speak it.

In my twenties, I couldn't have made the case for public speaking. While studying philosophy at university, I was devastated to find that the wonderful P. F. Strawson, a beautiful writer and brilliant thinker, was, at least on the day I heard him, a truly terrible speaker. He mumbled his way through 60 minutes, reading every sentence in the same monotone voice, barely looking up. I learned that I was utterly wasting my time going to his lectures when I could double down on just reading his books. So I stopped going to his lectures. In fact I stopped going to lectures, period. I just read.

One of the reasons I was so captivated by TED was the discovery that talks really can offer something more than the printed word. But it's not a given, and it's not even true in every case. That something extra has to be thought about, invested in, developed. It has to be earned.

What is that something extra? It's the human overlay that turns *information* into *inspiration*.

Think of a talk as two streams of input running parallel. Words are processed by your brain's language engine, which operates in much the same way when you're listening as when you're reading. But layered on top is a stream of metadata that allows you to (largely unconsciously) evaluate every piece of language you're hearing, determines what you should do with it, and how you should prioritize it. There's no analog to this in reading. It can only happen when you're watching a speaker and hearing her voice. Here are some of the impacts that the added layer can bring:

- Connection: *I trust this person.*
- Engagement: *Every sentence sounds so interesting!*
- Curiosity: *I hear it in your voice and see it in your face.*
- Understanding: *The emphasis on* that *word with* that *hand gesture — now I get it.*
- Empathy: *I can tell how much that hurt you.*
- Excitement: *Wow — that passion is infectious.*
- Conviction: *Such determination in those eyes!*
- Action: *I want to be on your team. Sign me up.*

In the aggregate, this is inspiration. Inspiration in its broadest sense. I think of it as the force that tells the brain what to do with a new idea. Many ideas just get filed away and probably soon forgotten. Inspiration, by contrast, grabs an idea and rushes it into our minds' attention spotlight: *General alert! Important new worldview incoming! Prepare to activate!*

There are many mysteries in how and why we respond so powerfully to certain speakers. These capabilities have evolved over hundreds of thousands of years and are deeply wired into us. Somewhere inside you there is an algorithm for trust. An algorithm for credibility. An algorithm for how emotions are spread from one brain to another. We don't know the details of those algorithms, but we can agree on important clues. And they break down into two big categories, what you do with your *voice* and what you do with your *body*.

SPEAK WITH MEANING

If you get a chance, listen to the opening minute of the TED Talk by George Monbiot. The text is charming, but not particularly sensational.

> When I was a young man, I spent six years of wild adventure in the tropics, working as an investigative journalist in some of the most bewitching parts of the world. I was as reckless and foolish as only young men can be. This is why wars get fought. But I also felt more alive than I've ever done since. And when I came home, I found the scope of my existence gradually diminishing until loading the dishwasher seemed like an interesting challenge. And I found myself sort of scratching at the walls of life, as if I was trying to find a way out into a wider space beyond. I was, I believe, ecologically bored.

But when he speaks, you hear something quite different. If I had to depict it just using typography, it would be something like this:

> When I was a young man, I spent *six years of wild adventure* in the tropics working as an **investigative** journalist in some of the most **bewitching** parts of the world. I was as reckless and foolish as only young men can be. This-is-why-wars-get-fought. But I *also* felt more a l i v e than I've ever done since. And when

I came **H O M E**, I found the scope of my existence gradually diminishing until **loading the dishwasher seemed like an interesting challenge.** And I found myself sort of *scratching* at the *walls* of life, as if I was trying to find a way OUT into a w i d e r space beyond. I was, I believe, **ecologically bored.**

In print, that looks awful. But when you hear Monbiot speak, you find yourself pulled instantly into his world. Almost every word he utters is crafted with a different layer of tone or meaning embedded in it, and the net effect is to add incredible nuance to his opening, nuance that print simply can't impart. That talent continues throughout the talk. The words he was uttering evoked intrigue and curiosity to be sure, but his *voice* practically forced you to feel curiosity and astonishment.

How did he do this? Voice coaches speak of at least six tools you can use: volume, pitch, pace, timbre, tone, and something called *prosody,* which is the singsong rise and fall that distinguishes, for example, a statement from a question. If you want to dig into these a little more, I thoroughly recommend a TED Talk by Julian Treasure called, "How to speak so that people want to listen." He not only explains what's needed, he offers exercises that help you get your own voice ready.

For me, the key takeaway is simply to inject variety into the way you speak, variety based on the *meaning* you're trying to convey. So many speakers forget this. They give a talk in which every sentence has the same vocal pattern. A slight rise at the start, and a drop at the end. There are no pauses or changes of pace. What this communicates is that no single part of your talk matters more than any other part. It's just plodding its way along until it gets to the end. The biological effect of this is hypnotic. That is, it simply puts your audience to sleep.

If your talk is scripted, try this: Find the two or three words in each sentence that carry the most significance, and underline them. Then look for the one word in each paragraph that *really* matters and underline it twice more. Find the sentence that is lightest in tone in the whole script and run a light wavy pencil line under it. Look for every question mark and highlight them with a yellow highlighter. Find the biggest single aha moment of the talk and inject a great big black blob right before it is revealed. If there's a funny anecdote somewhere, put little pink dots above it.

Now try reading your script, applying a change in tone for each mark. For example, let yourself smile while looking at the pink dots, pause for the big black blob, and speed up a little for the wavy pencil line, while speaking more softly. How does that sound? Really contrived? Then try again with a little more nuance.

Now try one more thing. Try to remember all the emotions associated with each passage of your talk. Which are the bits you're most passionate about? Which issues could make you a little angry? What are you laughing at? What are you baffled by? Now let *those* emotions out a little as you speak. How's it sounding? Try doing this with a friend present, and see what she responds to and what she rolls her eyes at. Record yourself reading it and then play it back with your eyes closed.

The point is to start thinking of your tone of voice as giving you a whole new set of tools to get inside your listeners' heads. You want them to understand you, yes, but you also want them to feel your passion. And the way you do that is not by *telling* them to be passionate about this topic, it's by showing your own passion. It spreads automatically, as will every other emotion you authentically feel.

You were worried about the short time limit? No worries. In a sense, you just doubled it. You can use every second not just to convey information but to communicate *how* that information might be received. And all without adding a single extra word.

For more great examples of the right use of voice, check out talks by Kelly McGonigal, Jon Ronson, Amy Cuddy, Hans Rosling, and the incomparable Sir Ken Robinson.

Some speaking coaches may push vocal variety beyond what feels right to you. Don't let them. Let it come naturally from the passion you feel for the topic. Mostly you want to speak conversationally, interjecting curiosity and excitement when it's appropriate. I ask people to imagine they've met up with friends they went to school with and are updating them on what they've been up to. It's that kind of voice you're looking for. Real, natural, but unafraid to let it rip if what you're saying demands it.

One other important aspect to pay attention to: how fast you're speaking. First of all, it's great to vary your pacing according to what you're speaking about. When you're introducing key ideas or explaining something that's complex, slow down, and don't be afraid to insert pauses. During anecdotes and lighter moments, speed up. But overall, you should plan to speak at your natural, conversational pace. For most speakers that's somewhere in the range 130–170 words per minute.

Some guides to public speaking urge people to deliberately slow down. In most circumstances, I think that's ill-advised. In general, understanding outpaces articulation. In other words, it usually takes the speaker's brain circuits more time to compose than the listener's to comprehend (*except* for the complex explanation moments, where yes, you should slow down). If you speak at your normal conversational pace, it's fine, the listener won't mind, but if you go much slower than that, you're inviting impatience into the room. Impatience is not your friend. While you're enjoying the biggest moment of your life, the audience is slowly dying of word starvation.

Rory Sutherland, who somehow maintained 17 minutes of hilarious, insightful speech at a rate of 180 words per minute, believes many speakers could benefit from speeding up a bit:

> There are two ways of losing an audience: going too fast is by far the rarer of the two. Going too slowly is actually the bigger problem, since it allows time for people's minds to wander off. I feel a bit guilty saying this, but if you speak quickly enough, you can get away with the odd leaping segue. I don't recommend blatant non sequiturs, obviously. Speaking fast also papers over a lot of cracks — no one minds or even notices the odd *um* or *er* provided they come quick and fast.

Neither he, nor I, is recommending that you rush or gabble. Just that you talk conversationally . . . and be ready to accelerate in passages where it's natural to do so. This works well, both in the room and online.

Does that surprise you? Do you think of public speaking as the opposite of conversational speaking?

At one TED conference, a first-time speaker from South Asia started his rehearsal bellowing at the top of his voice. I'm all for variety in speaking styles, but this was really exhausting to listen to. I asked him why he was speaking that way, and he thought for a moment and said, "In my culture, public speaking means speaking to a crowd of people. For the people at the back to hear, you have to shout. But," he paused, "but here, I suppose I do not need to do this, because here we have an automatic shouting device." He tapped his microphone and we burst into laughter.

It's actually a really important point. Public speaking evolved long before the age of amplification. To address a crowd of any size, speakers would have to slow down, breathe deep, and let rip, with dramatic pauses after each sentence. It's a style of speaking we recognize today as *oration*. It's a speaking style that can sync up crowd emotions and responses in a powerful way. We associate it with some of the most influential speeches in literature and history, from Marc Antony's "Friends, Romans, Countrymen" to Patrick Henry's "Give me liberty, or give me death!"

But in most modern settings, oration is best used sparingly. It's capable of conveying passion and urgency and outrage, but it struggles with the many more subtle emotions. And from an audience perspective, it can be really powerful for 15 minutes, but exhausting for an hour. If you were speaking to a single person, you would not orate. You could not build a day-long conference program around oration.

And oration is much slower. Martin Luther King's "I have a dream" speech was delivered at around 100 words per minute. It was perfectly crafted and delivered for its purpose. But it's unlikely that your task today is to address a crowd of 200,000 people at the heart of a major social movement.

Amplification has given us the ability to speak intimately to a crowd. It's an ability worth using. It builds connection and curiosity much more easily than oration. That conversational tone is even more important when you watch a talk online. There you're a single person looking at a screen, and you want the speaker to address you as such. Talks that are orated to a large crowd rarely go viral.

Some speakers fall into a trap here. In the thrill of being on stage, they get caught up in a slightly too grandiose sense of the occasion and begin unconsciously embracing a form of oration. They slow down their pace. They speak a little too loudly. And they insert dramatic pauses between sentences. This is an absolute talk killer. Oration is a subtle art that only a few are truly great at. It can be appropriate in church or at a mass political rally. But for other public-speaking occasions, I recommend leaving it alone.

RECRUIT YOUR BODY

Sir Ken Robinson jokes that some professors seem to view their bodies simply as devices to carry their heads into the next meeting. Sometimes a speaker will give the same impression. Once his body has moved his head onto the stage, it no longer knows what to do with itself. The problem is amplified in a setting where there's no lectern to hide behind. People stand awkwardly, hands glued to their sides, or lurch from leg to leg.

The last thing I want to do is prescribe a single approach to body language. Talks would quickly get boring if every speaker did the same thing. But there are a few things you can think about that may make you feel more comfortable, and that will better project your authority to your audience.

The simplest way to give a talk powerfully is just to stand tall, putting equal weight on both feet, which are positioned comfortably a few inches apart, and use your hands and arms to naturally amplify whatever you're saying. If the audience seating is curved around the stage a little, you can turn from the waist to address different parts of it. You don't have to walk around at all.

This mode can project calm authority; it is the method used by a majority of TED speakers, including Sir Ken. The key is to feel relaxed, and to let your upper body move as it will. Good posture helps; avoid slouching your shoulders forward. An open stance may feel vulnerable . . . but that vulnerability works in your favor.

Some speakers, though, prefer to walk the stage. It helps them think. It helps them emphasize key moments. This can work well too, provided the walking is relaxed, not forced. Take a look at Juan Enriquez in action. Or Elizabeth Gilbert. In both cases, they look extremely comfortable. And (this is important) they frequently stop to dwell on a point. It's that rhythm that lets this method work. Constant pacing can be tiring to watch. Pacing punctuated by stillness can be powerful.

Something to avoid is nervously shifting from leg to leg or walking forward and back a couple of steps in a kind of rocking motion. Many speakers do this without realizing it. They may be feeling a little anxious, and shifting from one leg to the other eases their discomfort. But from the audience's viewpoint, it actually highlights that discomfort. There have been so many times in TED rehearsals where we've encouraged these speakers to relax and to simply stand still. The difference in impact is immediate.

So, move if you want to. But if you do move, move intentionally. And then, when you want to emphasize a point, stop and address your audience from a stance of quiet power.

There are plenty of other ways you can speak with power. Dame Stephanie Shirley chose to sit for her talk, using a metal stool with one foot tucked back on a rung, and notes in her lap. It looked relaxed and natural. The late, great neurologist Oliver Sacks also sat for his talk. At the other end of the spectrum, Clifford Stoll leapt and darted around the stage with such energy that it added an entirely new and unique dimension to his talk.

So there are no rules here, other than for you to find a mode of being on stage in which you're comfortable and confident, and which doesn't detract from what you're saying. The simple test is to rehearse in front of a small audience and ask them if your body language is getting in the way, and/or video-record yourself to see if you're doing something you're unaware of.

The world can accommodate — and welcome — many different presentation styles. Just make sure your body knows it's not there solely to transport your head. It's allowed to enjoy its own time on stage.

DO IT YOUR WAY

And now, the most important lesson. It's an easy trap to get so caught up with the *how* of giving a talk that you forget what's more important, and that is — giving *your* talk in *your own* authentic way.

As with your wardrobe choice, once you've found a presentation style that works for you, don't overthink it. Don't try to be someone else. Focus on your content and your passion for it . . . and don't be afraid to let your own personality shine through.

The success of Jill Bolte Taylor's talk back in 2008 tempted a whole generation of TED speakers to try to imitate her emotional tone. That's a mistake. And it's one that Mary Roach almost fell for:

> The first thing I did upon being invited to give a talk was to click on the most popular TED Talk at that time, the one by Jill Bolte Taylor. I stopped it after 2 minutes, because I knew I could not be Jill Bolte Taylor. As insecure as I am, I knew it would be better to be Mary Roach than to be Mary Roach trying to be Jill Bolte Taylor.

Dan Pink agrees:

> Say it like yourself. Don't mimic someone else's style or conform to what you think is a particular "TED way" of presenting. That's boring, banal, and backward. Don't try to be the next Ken Robinson or the next Jill Bolte Taylor. Be the first you.

18

FORMAT INNOVATION

The Promise (and Peril) of
Full-Spectrum Talks

In November 2011, science writer John Bohannon took to the stage at TEDxBrussels, accompanied by an unusual speaking aid. Instead of PowerPoint, he brought with him a dance troupe. Actually, they brought him. They carried him onto the stage. And while he spoke about lasers and superfluids, they physically embodied the points he was making.

It was a riveting performance. Bohannon went on to argue that dance can be a great accompaniment for science talks, and he's even started a movement called Dance Your PhD.

If you want your talk to truly stand out from the crowd, there are many options open to you to be innovative.

If we look at the fundamentals, the only real constraint in a talk is the time available. In 18 minutes, you can utter about 2,500 words. But what else could you do? Your audience has five senses and is capable of absorbing multiple inputs.

At TED, we use the term *full spectrum* to describe those attempts to build more into a talk than just words and slides. Here are sixteen suggestions you could consider. We suspect we're going to see enormous innovation over the coming years.

Now, all of these need handling with extreme care. Done wrong, they can seem gimmicky. But done right, they can kick a talk up to a whole new level.

1. DRAMATIC PROPS

Twenty years ago I saw a talk about the need to continue to fight for nuclear disarmament. I can't remember the name of the speaker. Nor his organization. Nor much of what he said. But I will never forget what he did. He took a single dried pea and held it up. He said, "I want you to imagine that this is a thermonuclear weapon, a hydrogen bomb. It is one thousand times more powerful than the bomb dropped on Hiroshima." He tossed the pea into a large metal bucket that had a microphone attached to it. The scratchy ping when it landed and bounced was shockingly loud. Then he said, "And how many thermonuclear warheads do you think there are on Earth today?" He paused. "Thirty. Thousand." Without saying anything else he reached down and picked up a sack of dried peas, and tipped them into the bucket, first one at a time, then as a torrent. The sound was deafening, terrifying. At that moment, every person in that room understood deeply, viscerally, why this issue mattered.

Numerous TED Talks have been elevated by the use of unexpected props. To make a point about left and right brain hemispheres, Jill Bolte Taylor brought a real human brain onto the stage, complete with dangling spinal column. There was something about the relish with which she lifted it out of its bucket that stuck in everyone's mind. It was an object of passion! Bill Gates gained headlines across the world by releasing a jar full of mosquitoes during his talk on malaria, joking, "There's no reason why only poor people should have the experience." J. J. Abrams held us riveted by bringing on stage a mystery box his grandfather had given him that he'd never opened (and, of course, he left the stage with it still unopened).

If you have something you can powerfully, legitimately use, this can be a great way to make sure your talk is never forgotten.

But be careful. And be sure to practice in real-world conditions. I once brought a spectacular yellow Burmese python onto the stage, wrapped around my body, to make a point about nature's awesomeness. I thought I was rocking it . . . until the audience started guffawing. I didn't know that Burmese pythons are heat-seekers. The python had wriggled down my back and its head had just emerged, waving to and fro, from between my legs. Awesome, but not in quite the way I'd intended.

2. PANORAMIC SCREENS

At TED2015, MIT artist and designer Neri Oxman took everyone's breath away with a presentation featuring two parallel sets of images displayed simultaneously on giant screens that stretched out on either side of her. One revealed the tech side of her work; the other, the more organic side.

Each was impressive individually, the combination was absolutely stunning, but not just for its visual impact. It showed us, at a visceral level, the dual nature of her work as science-based designer and artist. The Google Zeitgeist conference is among those that have innovated ultra-widescreen presentations, allowing multiple versions of the same picture, spectacular panoramic photography, and bold lines of text stretching 100 feet on either side of the speaker. The cinematic feel of these presentations is incredible. (Trickier is how to edit them for online sharing. So far, the only mass-accessible formats are the standard video shapes of 16:9 and 4:3, so these presentations can be amazing in the room, but they are harder for an online audience to fully appreciate.)

3. MULTISENSE STIMULATION

Some speakers have sought to push beyond mere 2D vision and stereo sound. We've had chefs fill the hall with the delicious aroma of a dish being cooked live on stage. Or they have predistributed sample bags, allowing audience members to sniff and taste. Woody Norris showed us how his invention, hypersonic sound, could be projected from the stage to individual seats in the audience, where it was audible only to the occupants of those seats. Steve Schklair, a pioneer of 3D cameras, gave us an early demo of how sports could be experienced in 3D, courtesy of glasses distributed to all. Perfume designer Luca Turin used a machine to pump different scents into the room. These genre-busting talks are always interesting, but, with the possible exception of 3D, will probably remain limited to just a handful of topics.

However, at TED2015, David Eagleman made the case that exotic new senses could be added through technology, by training the brain to understand electrical patterns from any source, such as the weather or the stock market. Maybe some future conference will feature audiences wearing electrical vests, wired to directly experience a speaker's imagination. If anyone can invent *that*, please get in touch.

4. LIVE PODCASTING

One of the highlights of TED2015 was a talk by design guru Roman Mars. But instead of walking on stage with a microphone, Mars sat down behind a mixing console. He began, "I know what you're thinking: *Why does that guy get to sit down?* That's because . . . this is radio!" Cue music, and he's underway. Mars is the host of the popular design podcast 99% *Invisible*, and he gave the entire talk as if he were live-mixing his podcast. Numerous audio clips and images were mixed into the talk with split-second timing. This approach gave the talk incredible vitality. Superstar DJ Mark Ronson also used a mixing desk for parts of his talk. And

This American Life host Ira Glass mixes parts of his live shows from an iPad.

In truth, this technique is beyond the skills of most of us, but I can see it becoming an art form all its own. It's speaker-as-DJ, live-mixing ideas from multiple sources in real time. If you think this is a skill you could master, it might well be worth the time investment.

5. ILLUSTRATED INTERVIEW

An interview can be a fine alternative to a talk. This gives you a chance to

- explore multiple topics with no single throughline other than the speaker's work and life, and
- nudge the speaker to go deeper than he naturally would in a talk. (This is especially true with high-profile speakers, whose speeches are often written by their communications departments.)

At TED we've been experimenting with an interview format that encourages some preparation by both interviewer and interviewee, while still allowing for the in-the-moment cut and thrust of a traditional interview. It's a conversation *accompanied by a sequence of images* that has been worked out in advance by both parties. The images act as chapter markers for the various topics to be covered, and they add refreshing reference points for the conversation.

When I interviewed Elon Musk, I invited him to send me rarely seen videos illustrating key topics we wanted to talk about, such as his work on building reusable spacecraft. When the appropriate moment came, I simply played the relevant video and asked him to explain what we were looking at. It added pace and variety to the interview.

Likewise, when I was due to interview Bill and Melinda Gates about their philanthropic lives together, I asked them for photographs showing their early engagement in public health issues, any visual evidence of why they decided to become philanthropists, one key graph or image each that was meaningful to them, and — because we wanted to discuss the issue of inheritance — some pictures of their family. The images they came up with allowed us to make the interview much more personal than it otherwise could have been.

This format is a satisfying halfway point between talk and interview. It allows interviewees to really think about how they want to structure an idea that matters to them. And it decreases the risk of rambling or getting bogged down. I can picture lots of innovation here. For example, a talk, complete with slides, given informally by interviewee to interviewer, while the latter has the option to query any points that aren't clear, live on stage, while the talk is in progress.

6. SPOKEN WORD FUSION

A powerful art form emerged from African American communities in the 1970s and '80s and exploded into popular culture. *Spoken word* can be thought of as performance poetry; it typically combines storytelling with intricate wordplay. Spoken word artists offer an exciting extension of traditional public speaking. They don't seek to "explain" or "persuade" in the manner described in this book. Instead, they tap into a use of language that's more poetic, more primal; language that can energize, move, inform, and inspire.

There are many ways of blending the spoken word genre with public speaking. Sarah Kay, Clint Smith, Malcolm London, Suheir Hammad, Shane Koyczan, and Rives are among those who've given memorable performance-talks at TED. However, it's not something to take on lightly. Badly done spoken word can be excruciating!

7. VIDEOPOETRY EXPLORATION

The Canadian poet Tom Konyves defined videopoetry as a "poetic juxtaposition of images with text and sound." Online video has ignited an explosion of experimentation in video poetry, combining every imaginable mixture of text, live footage, animation, and spoken accompaniment. This is a genre capable of lighting up a talk. When former US poet laureate Billy Collins came to TED, he presented five of his works that had been set to video. Unquestionably, the animations enhanced the impact of his already powerful words. Shane Koyczan's spoken word performance at TED was enhanced by a video backdrop created by eighty crowd-sourced animators. There's huge potential in experimenting with videopoetry live, either as part of a talk or as an entire performance.

8. ADDED MUSICAL SOUNDTRACK

Why is it that almost every movie has a musical soundtrack? Music intensifies every emotion. It can indicate moments of special significance. It can dial up drama, sorrow, yearning, excitement, hope. So why not consider using it in talks?

Several speakers have experimented with this. When Jon Ronson told a chilling story about someone jailed as a suspected psychopath, Julian Treasure was behind him on stage creating an aural backdrop. *Pop Up Magazine,* which seeks to turn magazine content into live performance, regularly accompanies stories with a live string quartet or jazz trio, such as in the case of Latif Nasser, who told the amazing story of the man who invented modern pain relief.

The risk in going this route, apart from the intense extra effort needed in rehearsal, is that the form may reinforce the fact that this is performance, not an in-the-moment talk. This can be distancing. And in many settings, the introduction of music may feel emotionally manipulative.

Nonetheless, this seems to be fertile ground for experimentation. One route would be to incorporate musicians who can improvise based on what they're hearing live. Another would be to double down on the performance aspect and just make clear that this is how this particular talk is being delivered.

9. THE LESSIG METHOD

Law professor Lawrence Lessig has pioneered a unique style of presentation, a kind of PowerPoint on steroids. Every sentence and almost every significant word is accompanied by a new visual, whether just a word, a photograph, an illustration, or a visual pun. For example here's a single 18-second passage of his 2013 TED Talk, where each // represents a slide transition:

> Congress has evolved a different dependence, // no longer a dependence upon the people alone, // increasingly a dependence upon the funders. // Now this is a dependence too, but it's // different and conflicting // from a dependence upon the people alone // so long as // the funders are not the people. // This is a corruption. //

This shouldn't work. The blizzard of type changes in his slides seems to violate every design rulebook. But in Lessig's hands, it's riveting. There's so much intelligence and elegance in his choice of fonts, formatting, and images that you simply get swept along in awe. He told me the reason he started presenting this way was that he was sick of people at tech conferences looking down at their screens while he was speaking. He didn't want to give them a second to look away.

Lessig's presentation style is so startlingly different that some have given it its own name, the Lessig Method. If you're feeling bold, you could try emulating it. But be ready to spend a lot of time in preparation and rehearsal. And again, be careful. A lot of its brilliance is in the details and in the timing of the transitions. In the wrong hands, it can and will look clumsy and overbearing.

10. DUAL PRESENTERS

In general, we discourage talks given by more than one person. These somehow seem harder for audiences to connect to. They don't know who to look at, and they may never deeply relate to either presenter. But there are exceptions where the interaction between the two presenters adds real nuance. When Beverly and Dereck Joubert described their lifelong engagement with leopards and other wild cats, the clear affection and respect between them was touching in its own right.

I suspect there's plenty of room for innovation here. In most such dual presentations, when one of the speakers isn't talking, he is simply standing still or watching his partner. There are a lot of other possibilities:

- Gesturing
- Reenacting

- Accompanying with a musical instrument or percussion
- Sketching or painting
- Interjecting

If Lawrence Lessig had a twin brother, you could imagine them finishing each other's sentences in a way that would double the impact.

This is high risk. With two presenters, preparation is much more complex. Each individual is dependent on the other, and it's easy for their contributions and transitions to feel scripted. I don't recommend trying this unless you have incredible confidence and great chemistry with someone who it would be natural to experiment with. But I do think there's possibility here.

11. NEW DEBATE FORMATS

If you are going to have two people on stage at the same time, it's usually more interesting when they're on opposite sides of an issue. Often, the best way to really understand an idea is to see it challenged. There are numerous debate formats that offer exciting ways for this to happen. One of the best is an Oxford Union format, two against two. The speakers alternate with, say, 7-minute presentations for and against a controversial proposition. After moderator or audience engagement, they each have a 2-minute wrap-up, followed by an audience vote. (You can see this in action on the excellent website IntelligenceSquaredUS .org.)

But there are numerous alternatives, and I'd love to see innovation here. For example, you could try a courtroom format in which each "witness" is cross-examined by a skillful questioner. We're planning to introduce more debates to future TED events.

12. SLIDE BLIZZARD

Many talks by photographers, artists, and designers take the form of showing a sequence of slides and talking about each one. It's a good idea, but it's easy for people to dally too long on each slide. If your talent is primarily visual, you'll probably want lots of visuals, not lots of words. So it makes sense to dial up the number of slides and dial back the number of words devoted to each one.

There have been lots of attempts to systematize this. For example, at PechaKucha events, the talk format prescribes that 20 slides are shown with 20 seconds devoted to each one; the slides are advanced automatically, and the speaker has to keep up. Self-proclaimed "geek events," the Ignite talk series has a similar format, though in this case speakers' time is reduced to 15 seconds per slide. Both methods make for terrific, fast-moving events.

There's room to innovate further still. There's no reason why every slide should have exactly the same amount of time. I would love to see presentations that fit 100 slides into 6 minutes. Twelve could be "pause-and-talk" slides held for 20 seconds each, the rest could be shown in 1-second bursts and accompanied by a soundtrack or just silence.

13. LIVE EXHIBITION

The ultimate extension of the slide blizzard approach is to imagine that you're not giving a talk at all. Instead, you're creating the ultimate experience of immersion in your work. Suppose you're a photographer, artist, or designer who's been given a show in the main exhibition hall of one of the world's great art galleries. What would you want that experience to be? Imagine people moving from work to work, the lighting perfect, carefully created captions on each work to give them just the right amount of context. Now . . . why can't you re-create that experience live on stage?

Think of your words not as words from a talk, but as words designed to stir the right expectation or insight. They don't need to be sentences. They can be captions, signposts (words or phrases used to guide readers through the content of your essay), poetry. And they can be bracketed by silence. Yes, silence. When you have something incredible to show, the best way of drawing attention to it is to set it up, show it, and shut up!

As I mentioned previously, kinetic sculptor Reuben Margolin knows how to do this. During one 30-second period of his talk-cum-live-exhibition, here is all he had to say: "A single drop of rain increasing amplitude." Those words were surrounded by silence, but the screen was alive with the hypnotic movement of his sculpture, and the audience was lost in awe at the beauty he had created.

Photographer Frans Lanting created an entire performance around his photographs to illustrate the evolution of life on Earth. As the stunning photographs advanced, a Philip Glass soundtrack played, and Frans softly intoned life's story.

With all the tools available today in a modern theater — lighting, surround sound, hi-res projection — it's something of a tragedy that the world's best visual artists often don't make use of them. Instead of thinking about how to immerse an audience in their work, they assume that, since they were invited to give a *talk,* that's what they have to do. My hope for the future: more show, less tell.

14. SURPRISE APPEARANCES

After an extraordinary story is told about someone, there may be additional impact in bringing that person onto the stage live.

At TED2014, MIT professor Hugh Herr described how he had built a new bionic leg for Adrianne Haslet-Davis, a ballroom dancer who had been injured in the 2013 Boston Marathon bombing. Then he stunned the audience by introducing Adrianne live to give her first public dance performance on her new leg.

And at TEDxRíodelaPlata, Cristina Domenech's talk about poetry in prisons was energized by a live reading from inmate Martín Bustamante, who had been permitted a temporary release to attend.

This approach works best when there is a real contribution made by the special guest. If that can't happen, it's better simply to acknowledge his or her presence in the audience. To pull someone on stage for just a brief hello can feel awkward.

15. VIRTUAL PRESENTERS

Technology is allowing new ways to bring a speaker to the stage. In June of 2015, success coach Tony Robbins appeared at a business conference in Melbourne, Australia. Except he didn't want to actually travel all the way to Australia. So instead he appeared via 3D hologram. Organizers claim his avatar had as much impact as the man himself.

When we invited whistleblower Edward Snowden to TED in 2014, there was just one problem. He was living in exile in Moscow and couldn't travel to Vancouver for fear of being arrested. But we wired him in nonetheless in the form of a telepresence robot called BeamPro. If anything, it added to the drama. During the breaks, the Snowden bot roamed the hallway, allowing attendees to chat with him and snap photos (creating a Twitter trend #SelfiesWithSnowden).

Of course, both these uses benefited from their relative novelty. But the technology is continually improving. One of the surprises of TED's success has been that a speaker on video has almost as much impact as a speaker in the room. So there's no reason a hologram or telepresence bot can't have full impact.

The possibilities here are limitless. For example, when composer Eric Whitacre unveiled a piece of music at TED in 2013, it was performed not just by a choir on the stage. They were joined by musicians from thirty different countries, singing together live courtesy of a special tech hookup engineered for us by Skype. As they appeared onscreen, united in song, it seemed for a moment that the differences that tear our world apart could be bridged by elements as simple as an Internet connection, music from the heart, and people willing to reach out. I glanced around at the audience and saw many a cheek wet with tears.

I think we can expect to see a lot more experiments like this going forward. Innovations that will allow gatherings of people that simply wouldn't have been possible any other way. Indeed, there may well soon be a day when *real* robots walk on stage and give talks, talks that they have helped to write. (We're working on it!)

16. NO LIVE AUDIENCE

The ultimate talk innovation may be not to play with what happens on stage, but just to take away the stage altogether. Also, the theater, the live audience, and the host. After all, we're in a connected world now. Thanks to the Internet, we can communicate to countless thousands of people live or via video. That global audience can dwarf any group that can come together physically in a room. So why not just design a talk directly for that audience?

Swedish statistician Hans Rosling has done a series of incredible TED Talks, notching up collectively more than 20 million views. But one of his most popular talks wasn't done on a stage at all. It was filmed by the BBC in an empty warehouse, and Rosling's trademark graphics were added in postproduction.

In a world where everyone has access to video cameras and editing tools, there will be an unstoppable trend of significant talks delivered directly to the Internet. Our OpenTED initiative (described at the end of chapter 20) seeks to tap into this trend.

This won't replace the power of people coming together physically — there are far too many benefits from the ancient experience of real in-the-moment human contact. But direct-to-video talks will be a wonderful playground for rapid experimentation, innovation, and learning.

I am incredibly excited about the ways in which public speaking may evolve over the coming years. But I do also think it's worth sounding a note of caution. Many of the innovations mentioned above are potentially powerful, but they shouldn't be overused. The basic technology of human-to-human speaking goes back hundreds of thousands of years and is very deeply wired into us. In seeking modern variants, we must be careful not to throw out the baby with the bathwater. Human attention is a fragile thing; if you add too many extra ingredients, the main thrust of a talk may get lost.

So . . . let's embrace a spirit of innovation. There are wonderful opportunities out there to advance the great art of public speaking. But let's also never forget that substance matters more than style. Ultimately, it's all about the idea.

Reflection

19

TALK RENAISSANCE
The Interconnectedness
of Knowledge

I wish to persuade you of something: That however much public speaking skills matter today, they're going to matter even more in the future.

Driven by our growing connectedness, one of humankind's most ancient abilities is being reinvented for the modern era. I've become convinced that tomorrow, even more than today, learning to present your ideas live to other humans will prove to be an absolutely essential skill for:

- Any child who wants to build confidence.
- Anyone leaving school and looking to start a meaningful career.
- Anyone who wants to progress at work.
- Anyone who cares about an issue.
- Anyone who wants to build a reputation.
- Anyone who wants to connect with others around the world who share a passion.
- Anyone who wants to catalyze action to make an impact.
- Anyone who wants to leave a legacy.
- Anyone, period.

The best way I can make this argument is to share with you my own learning journey of the past couple of decades, a period that completely changed my understanding of why great public speaking matters, and what it might become. So let me take you back to Wednesday, February 18, 1998, Monterey, California, which is when and where I first set foot inside a TED conference.

Back then, I thought of conferences as necessary evils. You put up with hours of tedious panels and presentations in order to meet the people from your industry that you need to meet. However, my good friend Sunny Bates, one of the world's great connectors, persuaded me that TED was different and I should check it out.

I ended the first day a little bemused. I had heard a series of short talks from a software programmer, a marine biologist, an architect, a tech entrepreneur, and a graphic designer. They were nicely done. But I was struggling to find their relevance to *me*. I was a media guy. I published magazines. How was this going to help me to do my work better?

When TED was founded back in 1984, Richard "Ricky" Wurman and his cofounder, Harry Marks, had a theory that there was growing convergence between the technology, entertainment, and design industries (the *T, E,* and *D* of TED). It made sense. That was the year the first Apple Macintosh computer was launched, the year that Sony unveiled the first compact discs. Both products had deep roots in all three industries. It was exciting to imagine what other possibilities would emerge if you connected the three fields together. Maybe technologists could make their products more appealing by listening to the ideas of human-centered designers and creative entertainers? Maybe architects, designers, and entertainment-industry leaders could expand their sense of possibility by understanding new developments in technology?

And so it proved. After a wobbly start, and a personality clash between the founders (which persuaded Harry to sell his 50 percent stake to Ricky for a dollar), TED took off in the 1990s, accompanied by the rise of CD-ROM-fueled multimedia, *Wired* magazine, and the early Internet. In his earlier life, Ricky had coined the term *information architecture* and had become obsessed with making obscure knowledge accessible. This skill helped him drive speakers to find the most interesting angle on their idea, the angle that others outside their fields might enjoy or find relevant. And he had another personality trait that would obliquely prove core to TED's success: impatience.

Ricky easily became bored by long talks. As TED developed, he began giving speakers shorter and shorter time slots. And he simply walked on stage and cut people off if they went on too long. He also banned audience questions, on the grounds that it would be more interesting to cram in another speaker than hear some audience member promote his own business under the guise of asking a question. This may have been really annoying to a few individuals, but for the audience experience overall, it was a godsend. It made for a fast-moving program. You could put up with the occasional dud talk because you knew it would be over soon.

On my second day at TED, I began to truly appreciate the short-talk format. Even though I wasn't yet certain of the relevance to me and my work, I was certainly being exposed to a lot of topics. Video games for girls, the design of chairs, a new way of exploring information in 3D, a solar-powered airplane. They all followed each other in a rush. There was an exhilaration in learning how many different types of expertise there were in the world. And something was starting to spark. A comment made by a speaker in one field would somehow resonate with something someone in a completely different field had said the day before. I couldn't put my finger on it, but I was starting to get excited.

Most conferences serve a single industry or knowledge specialty. There, everyone has a common language and starting point, and it makes sense to allow speakers time to go really deep and describe some specific new learning. But when the content and audience are wide-ranging, a speaker's goal isn't to exhaustively cover a niche topic. Instead, it's to make her work accessible to others. To show why it's interesting. To show why it matters. That can usually be done in less than 20 minutes. And that's good, because for someone outside your field, that's probably all the time they'll give you. As listeners, we may be willing to invest 45 minutes or an hour on a university subject we have to learn, or on someone who works directly in our field. But to give someone outside our normal work life that kind of time? Not possible. There aren't enough hours in the day.

On day three, something really strange happened. My overstimulated brain began sparking like a lightning storm. Every time a new speaker got up and spoke, it felt like a new thunderbolt of wisdom. Ideas from one talk would connect in a thrilling way with something shared by others two days earlier.

And then came Aimee Mullins.

Aimee had had both her legs amputated at age one, but that hadn't stopped her from leading a full life. She sat on stage and spoke of how, three years earlier, as a college freshman, she had run her first race as a sprinter, and how, aided by a pair of beautifully designed sprinters' legs, she had rocketed through trials for the US Paralympics Team. And then she casually removed her prosthetics and showed how she could replace them easily with other legs for other situations.

As Aimee spoke about her surprising successes and embarrassing failures, I sat at the back of the theater, shocked at the tears running down my cheeks. She was so alive, and so full of possibility. She seemed to symbolize something I'd sensed time and again that week. That it was possible to own your future. No matter what life had served you, you could find a way to shape it, and in so doing make a difference for others too.

By the time I had to leave the conference, I understood why it meant so much to people there. I was thrilled by all I'd learned. I felt a greater sense of possibility than I had experienced in a long time. I felt like I'd come home.

Two years later, when I heard that Ricky Wurman was looking to sell the conference, I became tantalized at the thought of taking it over. For my entire entrepreneurial life, my mantra had been to follow the passion. Not my passion — other people's. If I saw something that people were truly, deeply passionate about, that was the big clue that there was opportunity there. Passion was a proxy for potential. That was how I justified launching dozens of hobbyist magazines, covering everything from computing to mountain biking to cross-stitching. Those topics might be deeply boring to most people, but to those the magazines were targeted at, they were passion-driven gold.

The passion I'd seen and experienced at TED was off the charts. People who had done amazing things with their lives had told me this was their favorite week of the year. So even though it was only a small annual conference, there was every possibility that something more could be built out of that passion.

On the other hand, it was a new business to get involved with, and I would be following in the shoes of a man with a much bigger, brasher personality than mine. What if I failed? The public humiliation would be pretty intense. I consulted friends, lay awake at night trying to imagine every possibility, but couldn't get to a decision.

What finally convinced me to go for it was, believe it or not, a passage in a book I happened to be reading at the time, namely David Deutsch's *The Fabric of Reality*. In it he asked a provocative question: Is it really true that knowledge has to become ever more specialized? That the only way we can achieve success is by knowing more and more about less and less? The specialization of every field — medicine, science, art — seemed to suggest this. But Deutsch argued convincingly that we must distinguish knowledge from understanding. Yes, knowledge of specific facts inevitably became specialized. But *understanding?* No. Not at all.

To *understand* something, he said, we had to move in the opposite direction. We had to pursue the *unification* of knowledge. He gave lots of examples in which older scientific theories were replaced by deeper, broader theories that tied together more than one area of knowledge. For example, an elegant worldview based on the sun sitting at the center of the solar system replaced massively complex explanations of the whirling motions of individual planets around Earth.

But more importantly still, Deutsch argued, the key to understanding anything was to understand the *context* in which it sat. If you imagine a vast spiderweb of knowledge, you can't really understand the intricate knots in any small part of that web without pulling the camera back to see how the strands connect more broadly. It's only by looking at that larger pattern that you can gain actual understanding.

I read this when I was dreaming about TED, and a light bulb flashed on. Of course! That was it! That was why the TED experience felt so thrilling. It was because the conference itself was reflecting the reality that all knowledge is connected into a giant web. TED truly did have something for everyone. We might not necessarily have realized it at the time, but by thinking about such eclectic ideas, we were all gaining understanding at a much deeper level than we had before. In fact, the individual ideas mattered less than how they all fit together — and what happened when we added them to our existing ideas.

So actually what made TED work was not really just the synergy between technology, entertainment, and design. It was actually the connectedness of *all* knowledge.

Framed that way, TED was an event that would never run out of things to talk about. How many venues were there where you could explore that connectedness? And explore it in a way that any curious person could find accessible and inspiring? I couldn't think of any.

I hopped on a plane to visit Ricky and his wife, Gloria Nagy, at their home in Newport, Rhode Island. And to cut a long and complicated story short, by the end of 2001, I had left the company I'd spent fifteen years building to become the proud, albeit slightly nervous, curator of TED.

In the years since then, I've become ever more convinced of the significance of the connectedness of knowledge, and I have encouraged TED to expand from the original *T-E-D* to pretty much every field of human creativity and ingenuity. I don't see this framing of knowledge and understanding as just a recipe for a more interesting conference. I see it as the key to us surviving and thriving in the brave new world that's coming. Here's how I'd make the case:

THE AGE OF KNOWLEDGE

Many of our assumptions about the value and purpose of knowledge and how to acquire it — including the structure of our entire education system — are leftovers from the industrial age. In that era, the key to success was for a company, or country, to develop massive expertise in production of physical goods. This required deep specialist knowledge: the geology required to locate and extract coal and oil; the mechanical engineering needed to build and operate industrial-scale machinery; the chemistry needed to efficiently produce a massive array of materials; and so forth.

The knowledge economy requires something different. Increasingly, the specialist knowledge traditionally wielded by humans is being taken over by computers. Oil is not located by human geologists but by computer software churning through vast amounts of geological data, looking for patterns. Today's best civil engineers no longer need to hand-calculate the stresses and strains on a new building; the computer model will do that.

Almost no profession is untouched. I watched an IBM Watson demo seeking to diagnose a patient with six specific symptoms. While doctors scratched their heads and ordered a range of tests to get more data, Watson, in just a few seconds, read through 4,000 recent relevant research papers, applied probability algorithms to each symptom, and concluded with 80 percent certainty that the patient had a rare condition only one of the human doctors had even heard of.

At this point people start getting depressed. They begin asking questions such as, *In a world in which machines are rapidly getting super-smart at any specialist knowledge task we can throw at them, what are humans even for?*

It's an important question. And the answer to it is actually quite thrilling.

What are humans for? Humans are for being more human than we've ever been. More human in how we work. More human in what we learn. And more human in how we share that knowledge with each other.

Our giant opportunity for tomorrow is to rise. To rise above our long history of using specialist knowledge to do repetitive tasks. Whether it's the backbreaking work of harvesting rice year after year or the mind-numbing work of assembling a product on a manufacturing line, most humans, for most of history, have made a living doing the same thing over and over again.

Our future won't be like that. Anything that can be automated or calculated ultimately will be. Now, we can be fearful of that, or we can embrace it and take the chance to discover a richer path to life fulfillment. What will that path look like? No one knows for sure. But it's probably going to include:

More system-level strategic thinking. The machines will do the grunt work, but we'll need to figure out how best to set them up to work effectively with each other.

More innovation. With the massive capabilities of a connected world available to us, there is huge advantage for those who can genuinely innovate.

More creativity. Robots will make a lot of our stuff, allowing for an explosion in demand for genuine human creativity, whether in tech invention, design, music, or art.

More utilization of uniquely human values. Human-to-human services will flourish, provided the humanity inherent in them is cultivated. It may be possible to develop a robotic barber, but will the service alone be enough to replace the chatty interaction with a great human hairstylist-cum-therapist? I doubt it. The doctor of the future may be able to ask for Watson's brilliance in diagnostic assistance, but that should allow more time for that doctor to really understand the human circumstances of her patient.

And, if any of that proves to be true, it's likely to require a very different type of knowledge than the industrial age asked of us.

Imagine a world where any piece of specialist knowledge is available to you instantly, on demand. If you have a smartphone, that's pretty much the world you're already living in. And if it isn't today, for your kids it will be. So what should we — and they — be learning for the future?

Instead of ever-greater amounts of ever-more-specialized knowledge, we're going to need:

- Contextual knowledge,
- Creative knowledge, and
- A deeper understanding of our own humanity.

Contextual knowledge means knowing the bigger picture, knowing the way all the pieces fit together.

Creative knowledge is the skill set obtained by exposure to a wide variety of other creative humans.

A deeper understanding of our own humanity comes not from listening to your parents or your friends, nor to psychologists, neuroscientists, historians, evolutionary biologists, anthropologists, or spiritual teachers. It comes from listening to *all* of them.

These types of knowledge aren't the domain of just a few professors in a few great universities. They aren't what you discover in a dominant company's apprenticeship program. This is knowledge that can only be assembled from a massive variety of sources.

And that fact, right there, is one of the main engines powering the renaissance in public speaking. We're entering an era where we all need to spend a lot more time *learning from each other*. And that means far more people than ever before can contribute to this collective learning process. Anyone who has a unique piece of work or a unique insight can productively participate. And that includes you.

But how? Whether you're a brilliant astrophysicist, a talented stonemason, or just a wise student of life, I don't need to learn from you everything you know. Of course not. That would take years. What I need to know is how your work connects to everything else. Can you explain the essence of it in a way I can understand? Can you share your work process in layman's terms? Can you explain why it matters? And why you are passionate about it?

If you can do this, you will expand my worldview. And you may do something else. You may spark new creativity or inspiration in me. Every field of knowledge is different, but they are all connected. And they often rhyme. This means that something in the way you describe your process may give me a crucial insight or catalyze a new thought in me. This is how ideas form when we spark off each other.

So the first great driver of the public-speaking renaissance is that the knowledge era we are entering demands a different type of knowledge, encouraging people to be inspired by those outside their traditional specialties, and in so doing to develop a deeper understanding of the world and their role in it.

But that's not all.

20

WHY THIS MATTERS

The Interconnectedness of People

The second great driver of the renaissance in public speaking is the epic technological shift that has given us all visibility to each other: the Internet, and in particular, the rise of online video. Let me tell the story as we experienced it, because in less than a year, online video flipped TED on its head and helped us become one of the pioneers of a new way of sharing knowledge.

A key catalyst for us was that TED is a nonprofit. We don't often think of nonprofits as robust vehicles for innovation, but in this case that status really helped. Let me explain.

When I was still working in magazines, I began to put money into a not-for-profit foundation in order to start giving back. It was that foundation that acquired TED. I work for it without drawing a salary. To me, removing the profit motive from the table sent a clear signal of intent. It made it much easier to credibly say to the world, *Come and help us build a new approach to discovering and sharing ideas.* After all, we ask attendees to pay a lot of money to come to our main conferences, and we ask speakers to come without being paid. It's much easier to do that if people can see that they're contributing to the public good as opposed to someone's personal bank balance.

How *should* TED best contribute to the public good? The small group of us running TED in the years after the transition pondered this question a lot. After all, TED was just a private conference. Yes, people were inspired there, but it was hard to see how you could scale that experience. Our early attempts to advance TED's nonprofit mission were to try a fellows program to bring to the event people who couldn't afford to pay,* to have a bigger focus on global issues, and to seek to turn inspiration into action with the introduction of the TED Prize, which granted its winners a wish to better the world that other attendees would support.

But at some point it felt like we had to find a way to share the *content* of TED. The ideas and insights being expressed deserved a broader audience. In early 2005 I found the perfect person to crack this problem. June Cohen had had an inside view of many of the key developments of the web. She was a key executive in the team that developed the pioneering HotWired website, which had the world's first online ads, and she had written a terrific book on what it took to create a successful website. Also, she'd begun coming to TED the same year I had, she'd fallen in love with it as I had, and every conversation between us had been provocative and valuable.

June joined our fledgling team and embarked on what seemed the logical strategy for sharing TED content more widely: get it on TV. Every TED conference ever held had been captured on video, and with all those cable channels out there, surely someone would be excited about airing a weekly show? We created a pilot, and June hawked it passionately to anyone who would listen. The resounding verdict from TV-land? *Meh.*

Talking heads make for boring TV — we heard that time and again. We tried suggesting that just possibly that boredom thing might not be about talking heads per se, but about talking heads saying boring things. We didn't get anywhere.

---

* Under Tom Rielly's leadership, the TED Fellows program has attracted more than four hundred fellows over the past ten years, a global network of talent that has energized every recent TED conference.

But meanwhile, something profound was happening to the world's infrastructure. Excited by the explosive growth of the Internet, telecom companies had decided to invest billions of dollars into fiber optics and other bandwidth upgrades. That enabled the liftoff of a technology that had at first seemed entirely innocuous: online video. During 2005, it morphed from a flickering novelty in the corner of a screen to something you could actually watch. A quirky little website called YouTube was launched, featuring short, user-generated videos, many of them starring kittens. Despite the amateurish look, it took off like a rocket.

In November 2005, June came to me with a radical suggestion. Let's deprioritize TV for now and try distributing TED Talk videos online instead.

On the face of it, that was a crazy idea. Quite apart from the still barely acceptable quality of online video, there was no proven revenue model for it. Could it really make sense to risk giving away our content? Wasn't that the only reason people paid so much to come to the conferences in the first place?

On the other hand, it would be a major step in advancing TED's nonprofit mission of sharing ideas for public benefit. And the thought of controlling our own distribution without dependency on TV networks was exciting. It was worth an experiment at the least.

Thus it was that, on June 22, 2006, the first six TED Talks debuted on our website. At the time, ted.com was getting about 1,000 visitors a day, most of them just checking details about past and future conferences. We dreamed that the release of these talks might kick that number up fivefold, yielding maybe 2 million talk views over a year, a massive boost in our overall reach.

The first day we had about 10,000 talk views. I assumed that, as usual with new media, after initial interest waned, the numbers would fall off quickly. The opposite happened. Within just three months we'd reached a million views, and the numbers just continued to climb.

Even more exciting was the tone of responses we were seeing. We had doubted the talks could have anything like the same impact online as they did live. After all, how could you hold someone's attention just peering at a small viewing window on a screen when there were so many other distractions online? The responses shocked and delighted us in their intensity: *Wow! Chills shooting down my spine! Cool and inspiring. The best presentation of a complex graphic I have ever seen. Tears running down my face . . .*

Suddenly it felt like the passion people experienced at the conference had been set free. And that could mean only one thing. The experiment we'd undergone releasing just a handful of TED Talks would have to be extended across all our best content. In March of 2007, we relaunched our website with a hundred talks available, and ever since then TED has been not so much an annual conference as a media organization devoted to "ideas worth spreading."

Oh, and that worry about us endangering the conference by giving away its content? Actually, the effect was the opposite. Our attendees were thrilled they could now share great talks with their friends and colleagues, and as word of TED Talks spread, the demand to attend the conferences actually rose.

Eight years later, interest in TED Talks has mushroomed globally. To our surprise and delight, it has become a global platform* for identifying and spreading ideas, thanks to the efforts of hun-

---

* The platform consists of physical events (the annual TED conference in Vancouver plus TEDGlobal, TEDYouth, TEDWomen, a corporate event series, various salons), the global TEDx movement of self-organized events, and numerous online channels (our own TED.com, but also YouTube, iTunes, *The TED Radio Hour* on NPR, mobile apps, and a broad range of collaborations with dozens of other organizations). There is a separate initiative aimed at students called TED-Ed, plus the annual TED Prize, and the TED Fellows program.

dreds of speakers, thousands of volunteer translators, and tens of thousands of local event organizers. As of late 2015, TED Talks are viewed some 100 million times every month — 1.2 billion times a year. It's not just TED, of course. Many other organizations also disseminate ideas in video format. Interest in online education generally has exploded. Khan Academy, MIT, Stanford University, and countless others have made available incredible resources for free to anyone in the world.

When you step back and ponder the implications, it's pretty thrilling. Consider it first from a speaker's point of view. Over history, many of the people most passionate about an idea have spent years crisscrossing a country or a continent trying to drum up audience interest. Realistically, the most successful anyone could hope to be at this would be to speak perhaps 100 times a year, in front of audiences of, on average, perhaps 500 people. So you might just about be able to reach 50,000 people in a year, and that would require a grueling schedule and an amazing advance publicity machine. Similarly, most authors selling a book about a serious idea would consider it a huge success if they sold 50,000 copies.

Yet online you can reach that many people in just your first day. And more than 1,000 speakers have gone on to reach an audience greater than 1 million people *for a single talk*. This represents a transformative leap in influence, and many speakers have attested to the impact it has made on their work.

But from a viewer's point of view, the implication is even more thrilling. Almost every human born at almost every place and moment in history has had their potential capped by a single fact over which they had almost no control, namely, the quality of the teachers and mentors they had access to. If a boy with Albert Einstein's brain had been born in Germany in the dark ages, there would have been no scientific revolution emanating from him. If a girl with Marie Curie's mind had been born in a remote Indian village twenty years ago, today she'd probably be harvesting rice and struggling to raise her children.

But now, for the first time in history, it's possible for anyone on the planet who has access to the Internet to summon to their home the world's greatest teachers and inspirers. The potential that represents is breathtaking.

And we should not think of this as a one-way process, speaker to listener. The most profound implication of online video is that it has created an interactive ecosystem in which we can all learn from each other. In fact, you might be surprised by the group of people I learned that idea from. Madd Chadd, Jay Smooth, Kid David, and Lil "C" are star members of the Legion of Extraordinary Dancers, the LXD. Their performance at TED in 2010 blew us all away. But even more astounding to me was that they had learned many of their skills by watching YouTube!

As their producer, Jon Chu, put it:

> Dancers have created a whole global laboratory online for dance, where kids in Japan are taking moves from a YouTube video created in Detroit, building on it within days, and releasing a new video, while teenagers in California are taking the Japanese video and remixing it with a Philly flair to create a whole new dance style in itself. And this is happening every day. From these bedrooms and living rooms and garages, with cheap webcams, come the world's great dancers of tomorrow.

YouTube had sparked a kind of global contest for dance innovation, causing the art form to evolve at breakneck speed. Chu had noticed this and had turned to YouTube as his main recruitment source for new dance talent. And the LXD were so breathtakingly good, they were chosen that year to perform at the Oscars.

As I listened to Chu and watched the LXD in action, it hit me that the exact same phenomenon was happening in public speaking. Speakers were watching each other's talks online and learning from each other, seeking to copy what was good, and then add their own unique innovations.

In fact you could see the same phenomenon at work in *any* skill that could be shared on video, from cake decorating to juggling. Online video was providing two things that had never before been available so potently:

- Visibility of the best talent in the world
- A massive incentive to improve on what was out there

The incentive was simply the thrill of becoming a YouTube star. The prospect of all those views, likes, and comments can motivate someone to slave away for hours or weeks, perfecting their own skills to be videoed and uploaded. If you spend any time on YouTube, you can discover thousands of niche communities, revolving around everything from unicycling to parkour to video poetry to Minecraft, teaching each other to do astonishing things.

This phenomenon demanded a name. I began calling it *crowd-accelerated innovation*. And by far its most exciting application is in the world of ideas.

For all of history, the vast majority of all talks given before an audience have remained invisible to all but those who were actually there. Today, for the first time, it's possible to go online and see thousands of different speakers in action, on almost any topic you care to name. It's possible to see how well their talks are regarded by looking at view counts, comments, etc., and therefore to filter down to the ones you most want to see.

So, suddenly we have an amazing laboratory at our disposal. And we also have a fantastic new incentive for millions of people to participate in this laboratory. If your best opportunity to give a talk is just for a few colleagues, or at a local club, you might not be that incentivized to really prepare. But now that what you say can be recorded and put online, that's different. Your potential audience is in the millions. Now how much time are you willing to put in?

This is a recipe for a glorious upward spiral of learning, innovating, sharing, and more learning. That is why I believe today's talk renaissance is only just getting underway. At TED, we've sought to nurture it in three main ways (in addition to sharing TED Talks on our site).

1. A TEDx EVENT NEAR YOU

In 2009, we began offering a free license to people who wanted to organize a TED-like event in their own town or city. We used the label *TEDx*, where *x* means it is independently organized and also signifies the multiplier effect of this program. To our delight, thousands of people have organized TEDx events. More than 2,500 are held every year in more than 150 countries. They have led to more than 60,000 TEDx talks being uploaded to YouTube. And a growing number of those talks have gone viral. If you don't think you can give the talk you want to give at work, you could consider reaching out to your local TEDx organizer. There might be the perfect stage waiting in your own neighborhood.*

2. A KIDS' PROGRAM FOR PRESENTATION LITERACY

We launched a free program for schools called TED-Ed Clubs that allows any teacher to offer a group of kids a chance to give

---

* You can locate your closest events or apply to organize an event of your own at http ://ted.com/tedx.

their own TED Talk. A session once a week for thirteen weeks encourages selection of an idea, tips on how to research it, and then the skills to prepare and deliver the talk. The boost to the confidence and self-esteem of kids who make it through to the delivered talk is inspiring to see. We think presentation literacy should be a core part of every school's curriculum, on par with reading and math. It's going to be an important life skill to have in the decades ahead.*

3. UPLOAD YOUR OWN TED TALK

We have a program called OpenTED that allows anyone to upload their own TED-like talk to a special section on our site. We specifically encourage innovation, not just in content but in how the talk is given. We're betting someone out there will hit on a beautiful new way to share ideas. Perhaps it will be you.†

And over the next decade, as several billion more people get online, we're excited at the prospect of reaching out to them and offering a means to learn from the great teachers who can empower them to achieve a better life, and to share their unique insights and ideas with the rest of us. The prospect of a world population growing to 10 billion over the coming thirty years is daunting. But it's a lot less so if you imagine that it will bring not just more consumption, but also more wisdom.

The revolution in public speaking is something everyone can be part of. If we can find a way to truly listen to each other, and learn from each other, the future glitters with promise.

---

* The TED-Ed Clubs program is housed at http://ed.ted.com.
† Details on how to upload your talk are at http://open.ted.com.

21
YOUR TURN
The Philosopher's Secret

My father was a missionary eye doctor. He devoted his life to trying to cure blindness in Pakistan, Afghanistan, and Somalia, while simultaneously trying to spread the Christian gospel. It's probably a good thing he never got to see one of the first speakers I brought to the TED stage. That was philosopher Dan Dennett, an avowed atheist. They would have disagreed pretty much across the board. Except on one thing.

Halfway through a riveting talk on the power of memes, Dennett said this: "The secret of happiness is: find something more important than you are, and dedicate your life to it."

That is a statement my father would have profoundly agreed with.

Dennett is a passionate advocate for the power of ideas. He was highlighting an extraordinary fact about humans, one that's unique to our species: we are sometimes willing to subjugate our biological needs for the pursuit of ideas that matter. And in Dennett's view — and my father's, and mine — that pursuit is one of the keys to a meaningful, satisfying life.

We're strange creatures, we humans. At one level, we just want to eat, drink, play, and acquire more stuff. But life on the hedonic treadmill is ultimately dissatisfying. A beautiful remedy is to hop off it and instead begin pursuing an idea that's bigger than you are.

Now, in your case, I of course don't know what that idea is. And maybe, right now, you don't either.

Maybe you want to highlight an invisible community in your town, or do some historical research into a family member whose courage should be better known, or organize cleanup days in your community, or delve into marine science, or get active in a political party, or build a new piece of technology, or travel somewhere where human needs are a hundred times greater than anything you've faced, or just tap into the experience and wisdom of the people you meet.

Whatever it is you pursue, if you truly go after it, I predict two things:

- Yes, you'll find a meaningful form of happiness.
- You'll discover something that matters far more than any piece of advice you've read in this book: you'll discover *something worth saying.*

And then what? Well, then, of course, you must *share* it, using all the passion, skills, and determination you can muster. Share it in the way that ultimately only you will know how to do. Start a fire that will spread new wisdom far and wide.

Tom Chatfield is a technology commentator who spoke at one of our events. My colleague Bruno Giussani asked him for his advice for other speakers. This is what he said:

The most amazing thing about a talk, for me, is its potential for impact. The short talk you're about to give has the potential not only to reach hundreds of thousands of people, but to start many thousands of conversations. And so the central advice I would give is to push yourself as hard as possible to be bold and brave, to try to step outside the comfort zone of what you know for sure or what others have said already, and to give the world questions and inspirations that deserve a thousand conversations. It's not about being right, or safe — it seems to me — so much as about having a staggering opportunity to create something that will breed further ideas.

I love that quote. I want a future in which people realize their potential to nudge the world. Seeding a valuable idea, I am convinced, is the most impact that's possible for an individual to have. Because, in a connected world, that idea, once properly seeded, is capable of spreading itself. There's no limit to the number of people it can influence, both now and in the future.

But what about those who would nudge the world in a bad direction? Can't public speaking be used for harm as well as good?

It can. From demagogues to soul-destroying cynics, there's plenty of painful evidence of this.

However, I don't think there's complete symmetry here. There are strong reasons to believe that the accelerating growth of spoken content is going to tilt positive. Let me explain.

As we've learned, to give an effective talk, a speaker has to go to where a listener is and say, *Come, let's build something together.* The speaker must show why the idea is worth building. There is a reaching out. An appeal to shared values, desires, hopes, and dreams.

In certain circumstances this process can be terribly abused. A crowd can be whipped up. Hatred inflamed. False views of the world can be propagated as real. But in history this has always happened when, at least to some degree, listeners are shut off from the rest of the world. The appeal that is being made by the speaker is not universal, it is tribal. It is us versus them. And crucial facts are hidden from these listeners.

But when we're more closely connected — when people have

full visibility of the world and each other — something different starts to happen. Then, the speakers who will have the most influence will be those who succeed in tapping into those values and dreams that are most widely shared. They will be those who use arguments based on facts that many people — not just a few — can see to be true.

Imagine two religious speakers who want to influence the entire world. One of them speaks of the superiority of his own religion over all others and urges mass conversion. The other notices that the single deepest value of his religion, compassion, is also shared by every other religion. He decides he will speak on that, and he makes an effort to speak in universal terms that those from other religions will respond to and will be moved by. Which of those speakers has the bigger potential audience and long-term impact?

Or imagine two global political leaders, one of whom appeals only to the interests of one race, while the other reaches out to all members of humanity. Which one garners more support in the end? If it were the case that humans were irredeemably xenophobic, close-minded, racist, then to be sure the second politician would have no hope. But I don't believe that to be the case. I believe that what we share is far more meaningful, more profound, than how we differ. We all hunger, yearn, suffer, laugh, weep, and love. We all bleed. We all dream. We are all capable of empathy, of putting ourselves in others' shoes. And it is possible for visionary leaders — or anyone with the courage to stand up and say something — to tap into this shared humanity and to nurture it.

I spoke earlier of the power of reason over the very long term. Reason, by its very nature, seeks to look at the world not from an individual perspective but from the perspective of all of us. Reason rejects arguments that say "I want this to happen because it's in my interest" in favor of "Here's why we should *all* want this to happen." If reason didn't do this, it could never have become the common currency of discussion that allows humans to align. When we say *Be reasonable,* this is exactly what we mean. We're saying, *Please look at the issue from a broader perspective.*

The power of reason, combined with the growing connectedness of the world, tilts the balance of influence in favor of speakers who are willing to put themselves in the shoes of all of us, not just the other members of their own tribe. The latter may have their moments of power, but it is the former who will win in the end.

That is why I deeply believe in Martin Luther King Jr.'s shining statement: "The arc of the moral universe is long, but it bends towards justice." There really is an arrow to history. There really is such a thing as moral progress. If we pull the camera back for a moment, away from whatever evil du jour is dominating the news, we can see that progress writ large in the history of the last few centuries, not least in the impact of MLK himself. And it has every chance of continuing.

As humans continue to be brought closer, not just by technology but by an ever deeper understanding of each other, so we will find more ways of seeing in each other the things we mutually care about. And that is how barriers come down and human souls unite.

It won't happen quickly, nor easily. This type of change is multigenerational. And there are plenty of imaginable disasters that could blow it off course. But at least we have a shot.

Talking with each other is a crucial part of nurturing that change. We're wired to respond to each other's vulnerability, honesty, and passion — provided we just get a chance to see it. Today, we have that chance.

In the end, it's quite simple. We are physically connected to each other like never before. Which means that our ability to share our best ideas with each other matters more than it ever has. The single greatest lesson I have learned from listening to TED Talks is this: *The future is not yet written. We are all, collectively, in the process of writing it.*

There's an open page — and an empty stage — waiting for your contribution.

ACKNOWLEDGMENTS

Like all ideas, those offered in this book have many parents.

I have spent endless hours with my close colleagues at TED, especially Kelly Stoetzel, Bruno Giussani, and Tom Rielly, trying together to understand the essence of a great TED Talk. This book is theirs as much as mine.

We've had access to many of the world's best thinkers and speakers, whose wisdom we've greedily sought on the significance of ideas and on every aspect of turning them into memorable words. A special call-out to Steven Pinker, David Deutsch, Sir Ken Robinson, Amy Cuddy, Elizabeth Gilbert, Dan Pallotta, Daniel Kahneman, Bryan Stevenson, Dan Gilbert, Lawrence Lessig, Amanda Palmer, Pamela Mayer, Brené Brown, Allan Adams, Susan Cain, Steven Johnson, Matt Ridley, Clay Shirky, Daniel Dennett, Mary Roach, Rory Sutherland, Sarah Kay, Rives, Salman Khan, and Barry Schwartz. Actually, we've learned from every single speaker who's appeared at TED, and we feel immense gratitude to them for the gift they've given us all. Thanks too to our three favorite speaker coaches: Gina Barnett, Abigail Tenembaum, and Michael Weitz.

Many long-standing members of the TED community have been wonderfully supportive over the past fifteen years and have helped us imagine what TED might become. Scott Cook,

Sunny Bates, Juan Enriquez, Chee Pearlman, Tim Brown, Stewart Brand, Danny Hillis, Cyndi Stivers, Rob Reid, Arch Meredith, Stephen Petranek . . . you rock! And there are so many more.

Some of the world's busiest people somehow found the time to read an early manuscript and offer invaluable advice, including Helen Walters, Michelle Quint, Nadia Goodman, Kate Torgovnick May, Emily McManus, Beth Novogratz, Jean Honey, Gerry Garbulsky, Remo Giuffre, Kelo Kubu, Juliet Blake, Bruno Bowden, Rye Barcroft, James Joaquin, Gordon Garb, and Erin McKean.

Warm thanks to my miracle-weaving agent, John Brockman, my brilliant editor, Rick Wolff (who is vetoed from deleting *this* use of *brilliant* even if he was right to take out most of the others), my tireless copy editor, Lisa Sacks Warhol, and the whole team at Houghton Mifflin Harcourt. It's been a pleasure to work with all of you.

Richard Saul Wurman, none of this would have happened without you. June Cohen, thank you for eleven years at TED and for guiding the first TED Talks onto the Internet. Mike Femia and Emily Pidgeon, thanks for design guidance. To the entire team at TED, wow, just *wow*. You amaze me with all you do. Susan Zimmerman, you especially!

To our army of volunteer translators, thank you for taking TED Talks to the world. To the tens of thousands of TEDx volunteers, I'm awed by the passion and brilliance that goes into each event that you organize. To the global TED community . . . ultimately, this is all down to you. Without you, thousands of significant ideas would have remained unspread.

To my extraordinary daughters, Elizabeth and Anna, you have no idea how proud I am of you; nor how much I have learned from you. And finally, to the force of nature I'm married to, Jacqueline Novogratz . . . thank you, a million times thank you, for your love and your inspiration, every single day.

TALKS REFERENCED
WITHIN THE BOOK

These are available on a single playlist at:
www.ted.com/tedtalksbook/playlist

PAGE(S)	SPEAKER	TED TALK TITLE
4	Monica Lewinsky	The price of shame
6–8	Chris Anderson	TED's nonprofit transition
11	Sophie Scott	Why we laugh
33	Robin Murphy	These robots come to the rescue after a disaster
49, 203	Kelly McGonigal	How to make stress your friend
50–51, 174	Brené Brown	The power of vulnerability
51–52	Sherwin Nuland	How electroshock therapy changed me
53, 203	Ken Robinson	Do schools kill creativity?
57–58	Dan Pink	The puzzle of motivation

PAGE(S)	SPEAKER	TED TALK TITLE (CONT.)
59–60	Ernesto Sirolli	Want to help someone? Shut up and listen!
68–69	Eleanor Longden	The voices in my head
69	Ben Saunders	To the South Pole and back — the hardest 105 days of my life
69, 140	Andrew Solomon	How the worst moments in our lives make us who we are
72–77	Dan Gilbert	The surprising science of happiness
81	Deborah Gordon	The emergent genius of ant colonies
83	Sandra Aamodt	Why dieting doesn't usually work
83, 203	Hans Rosling	Let my dataset change your mindset
83	David Deutsch	A new way to explain explanation
83	Nancy Kanwisher	A neural portrait of the human mind
83	Steven Johnson	Where good ideas come from
83	David Christian	The history of our world in 18 minutes
83–85	Bonnie Bassler	How bacteria "talk"
86–87	Steven Pinker	The surprising decline in violence
88–89	Elizabeth Gilbert	Your elusive creative genius
89	Barry Schwartz	The paradox of choice

91–92, 95	Dan Pallotta	The way we think about charity is dead wrong
98–99	David Gallo	Life in the deep oceans
102, 103–104	Jeff Han	The radical promise of the multi-touch interface
103	Markus Fischer	A robot that flies like a bird
158	Maysoon Zayid	I got 99 problems . . . palsy is just one
158	Jamie Oliver	Teach every child about food
158–159	Zak Ebrahim	I am the son of a terrorist. Here's how I chose peace
159–160	Alice Goffman	How we're priming some kids for college — and others for prison
160	Ed Yong	Zombie roaches and other parasite tales
161–162	Michael Sandel	Why we shouldn't trust markets with our civic life
162	V. S. Ramachandran	3 clues to understanding your brain
162	Janna Levin	The sound the universe makes
163	Alexa Meade	Your body is my canvas
163–164	Elora Hardy	Magical houses, made of bamboo
169–170	David Eagleman	Can we create new senses for humans?
170, 203	Amy Cuddy	Your body language shapes who you are

PAGE(S)	SPEAKER	TED TALK TITLE (CONT.)
170–171, 203	Jon Ronson	When online shaming spirals out of control
171	Bill Stone	I'm going to the moon. Who's with me?
171–172	Diana Nyad	Never, ever give up
172	Rita Pierson	Every kid needs a champion
173	Esther Perel	Rethinking infidelity . . . a talk for anyone who has ever loved
173	Amanda Palmer	The art of asking
174–175	Bryan Stevenson	We need to talk about an injustice
200–201	George Monbiot	For more wonder, rewild the world
212	Roman Mars	Why city flags may be the worst-designed thing you've never noticed
216–217	Lawrence Lessig	We the People, and the Republic we must reclaim
220	Reuben Margolin	Sculpting waves in wood and time
243	The LXD	In the Internet age, dance evolves . . .
247	Dan Dennett	Dangerous memes

INDEX

Aamodt, Sandra, 83
Abrams, J. J., 166, 210
acknowledgments, 26, 123, 156–57,
    168, 253–54
adrenaline rush, 183, 185–86
aesthetic appeal, 118–19
Anderson, Chris
    bio of, 37–39, 247
    first TED for, 228–30
    TED leadership, 6–8, 12, 231–33
anecdote usage, 55–56, 94
art visuals, 98, 99–100, 118–19, 163–64,
    219–20
articulation, 203
assumptions
    curse of knowledge, 78–82
    persuasive demolition of, 86–87,
        88
attention war, 157, 167
audience
    compassion fatigue of, 41
    connection permission, 47–48
    eye contact with, 48–50, 187, 193, 194
    journey experience of, 20–21, 33, 48,
        93, 148
    knowledge base of, 71, 78–82
    language choice for, 17–18
    as person, 42–43, 187
    questions from, 229
    rehearsal, 149
    standing ovation from, 26–27
    virtual, 222–23
audio
    full-spectrum formats, 212–13
    music, 215–16, 222
    testing, 126
authenticity
    in humor, 56
    imitation of, 26–29, 208
    in narration, 61
    naturalness and, 130–31, 133, 136–39,
        141, 145
    power of, 10, 13–14
    reading from script and, 132, 134,
        136, 140, 189, 194–96
    stage presence, 207, 208
    vulnerability and, 52–53
autocues, 195–96

backup plan, 187, 191
Barry, Drew, 129
Bassler, Bonnie, 83–85
Bates, Sunny, 228
Bezos, Jeff, 8

biases, 74–75, 78–82
Blair, Tony, 58
body care for nerves, 185–86
body language
    eye contact, 48–50, 187, 193, 194
    hiding, 190
    overemphasis of, 19–20
    power posing, 170, 185
    stage presence, 206–7, 209
Bohannon, John, 209
Bolte Taylor, Jill, 148, 208, 210
Bono, 195
Botsman, Rachel, 149
breathing, 185
Brown, Brené, 37, 50–51, 52–53, 174
business presentations, 25–26, 101–2
Bustamante, Martín, 221

Cain, Susan, 149
call to action, 170–71
charisma, 13, 19, 29
charity reform, 90, 91, 95
Chatfield, Tom, 248–49
Chevalier, Tracy, 152–53
choice, paradox of, 88, 89–90
Christian, David, 83, 164
Chu, Jon, 243
Cliatt-Wayman, Linda, 180
clichés, 28, 161, 168
closing
    bad, 168–69
    call to action, 170–71
    camera pull-back, 169–70
    encapsulation, 173
    lyrical, 174–75
    narrative symmetry, 173
    personal commitment, 171–72
    values and vision, 172
clothing, 179–82
cognitive biases, 74–75, 78–82
cognitive load, 115–16

Cohen, June, 41, 239
Collins, Billy, 215
commitment, personal, 171–72
compassion fatigue, 41
comprehension. See understanding
conceptualizing. See explanation
confidence, 13–14, 133, 147, 179
confidence monitors, 193–95
connection
    ancient, x–xi, 63–64
    ego removal for, 57–59
    eye contact for, 48–50, 187, 193, 194
    humor for, 8, 53–57, 58
    of knowledge, 227–33, 242–45
    narration for, 59–61
    of people, 242–45, 249–52
    permission for, 47–48
    reading from script and, 132, 134,
        136, 140, 189, 194–96
    vulnerability for, 50–53, 190
connection killers, 61–62. See also talk
    styles to avoid
contextual knowledge, 232, 235
conversational speaking, 10, 139–41,
    152, 169–70, 203–5
creative genius, 88–89
creative knowledge, 236
credits, photo, 122–23
Cuddy, Amy, 6, 110, 170, 185
curiosity
    on heavy topics, 41, 93, 163
    as opening hook, 160–63
    on tough concepts, 72, 74, 76, 83–84,
        162–63
curse of knowledge, 78–82

da Vinci, Leonardo, 92–93
data visualization, 116–17, 118
Davis, Fred, 196
de Gaulle, Yvonne, 8
debate format, 218

delivery. *See also specific formats;* notes;
    scripted talks; talk styles to avoid;
    unscripted talks
  body language in, 19, 206–7, 208
  charismatic, 13, 19, 29
  confidence in, 13–14, 133, 147, 179
  forgetting, 130–31, 143–144, 145, 187,
      188
  naturalness of, 130–31, 132, 136–39,
      141, 145
  pitfalls, 131–32
  rambling, 24–25, 68, 144, 152
  transitions in, 124–25, 151, 204
  voice in, 198–205, 208
demonstrations, 102–4, 212
Dennett, Daniel, 89, 90, 247
Descartes, 90
detective storytelling, 92–93
Deutsch, David, 83, 231–32
Domenech, Cristina, 221
drama
  as opening hook, 157–60
  props for, 210–11
dramatic prop format, 210–11
dreams of future, 105–9, 172, 234–35
dual presenters, 217–18
Dugan, Regina, 108

Eagleman, David, 169–70, 212
Earle, Sylvia, 107
Ebrahim, Zak, 158–59
education reform, 32, 107, 172, 242,
      245–46
ego, 36–37, 41, 57–59, 169, 249–51. *See
    also* talk styles to avoid
emotions
  communicating, 19, 200–201, 202,
      205
  manipulating, x, 27–29, 52–53, 60, 216
empathy, 41, 64, 107, 250
encapsulation, 173

Enriquez, Juan, 109, 206
example usage, 73, 75, 77, 94
exercise, 186
exhibitions, live, 219–20
experience simulation, 73–74, 107
explanation
  core elements of, 76–77
  curse of knowledge and, 78–82
  jargon in, 81–82
  key examples of, 72–76, 83–85
  phrasing for, 80–81
  structure and throughline for, 79–80
  understandability of, 77–81, 100,
      115–16
  visuals for, 115–18, 122
  of what isn't, 82
exploration talks, 98–102, 166
eye contact, 48–50, 187, 193, 194

Fabric of Reality, The (Deutsch), 231–32
fear response, 3, 183. *See also*
      nervousness
Ferren, Bran, 108–9
Fischer, Markus, 103
fMRI. *See* functional magnetic
      resonance imaging
fonts, 120–21, 122
forgetting talk, 130–31, 143–144, 145,
      187, 188
functional magnetic resonance imaging
      (fMRI), 18
future visions, 105–9, 172, 234–35

Gallo, David, 98–99
Gates, Bill, 153, 210, 214
Gates, Melinda, 214
generosity, 24
genius, 88–89
Gilbert, Dan, 72–76, 139–40, 146
Gilbert, Elizabeth, 42–43, 88–89,
      143–44, 206

Giussani, Bruno, xiii, 25, 30, 248
Gladwell, Malcolm, 70
Glass, Ira, 213
Goffman, Alice, 159–60
Goldstein, Rebecca Newberger, 96
Google Zeitgeist, 211
Gordon, Deborah, 81
Gore, Al, 61–62
Gowdy, Barbara, 188
guest appearances, 220–21
Gutman, Ron, 49

Hammad, Suheir, 215
Han, Jeff, 102, 103–4
happiness, 8, 72–76, 88–90, 247–48
Hardy, Elora, 163–64
Haslet-Davis, Adrianne, 221
Hasson, Uri, 18
Heatherwick, Thomas, 108
Hembrey, Shea, 99
Herr, Hugh, 221
human element. *See also* psychosocial
    phenomena
  in age of knowledge, 234–36
  interconnectedness, 242–45,
      249–52
  in voice, 199
humor
  for connection, 8, 53–57, 58
  for reasoning, 94

IBM Watson, 234, 235
idea-building. *See also* talk tools;
    throughlines
  importance of, xiv–xv, 6, 10, 12–13,
      188, 248–49
  language power of, 17–19
  simplification of, 32, 36–37, 82, 115–16
ideas
  defining, 12–13
  issues vs., 41

pursuit of, 13–16, 32, 247–48
  structure around, 39–41
if-then reasoning, 91
imitation, 26–29, 208
impact bias, 74–75
impressions
  closing, 168–75
  opening, 156–67
  wardrobe and, 179–82
improvisation. *See* unscripted talks
Inconvenient Truth, An, 61–62
inspiration
  information into, 199
  performing, 26–29
Internet impact, xi–xii, 221–23, 238–45
interviews, illustrated, 213–14
intuition pumps, 89–90
invention talks, 102–4, 166
iPads, 193
Isay, Dave, 109
issues, ideas vs., 41

jargon, 81–82, 100
Jobs, Steve, 148
Johnson, Steven, 83, 145, 173–74
Joubert, Beverly and Dereck, 217
journey experience, 20–21, 33, 48,
      93, 148

Kahneman, Daniel, 133, 168, 190
Kamkwamba, William, 6
Kanwisher, Nancy, 83
Kay, Sarah, 215
Kennedy, John F., 106
Khan, Salman, 32, 57, 107, 110, 145, 150
Kidd, Chip, 181
kids' programs, 245–46
King, Martin Luther, Jr., 105–6, 205, 251
knowledge
  age of, 233–37
  audience's base of, 71, 78–82

curse of, 78–82
gaps, 74, 76, 81, 161
interconnectedness of, 227–33,
    242–45
specialization, 231–32, 233–34
types of, 235–36
understanding vs., 231–32
Konyves, Tom, 215
Kowan, Joe, 188
Koyczan, Shane, 215

language. *See also* body language
    jargon, 81–82, 100
    lyrical, 136, 139–40, 174–75, 214–15
    power of, 17–19, 199–200
    scripting choice of, 139–40
    spoken word fusion, 214–15
Lanting, Frans, 220
Larson, Kent, 108
laughter, 11, 53–54
learning
    education reform for, 32, 107, 172,
        242, 245–46
    Internet impact on, 236, 242–45
Learning Wednesdays, 16
lecterns, 189–91, 196–97
lectures, 198
Ledgett, Richard, 186
Legion of Extraordinary Dancers
        (LXD), 243
Lessig, Lawrence, 70, 216–17
Lessig Method, 216–17
Levin, Janna, 162
Lewinsky, Monica, 4, 54, 183–85, 196–97
Li, Fei-Fei, 166
listening
    evolution of, 64
    power of, 18–19, 199–200
    reading vs., 198–201
literacy, presentation, xii, 10, 245–46
London, Malcolm, 215

Longden, Eleanor, 68–69
Lovegrove, Ross, 101
LXD. *See* Legion of Extraordinary
        Dancers
lyricism, 136, 139–40, 174–75, 214–15

Macaulay, David, 100–101
manipulation, x, 26–29, 52–53, 60,
    216
Mancini, Pia, 49
Margolin, Reuben, 101, 220
Marks, Harry, 228
Marks, Nic, 37
Mars, Roman, 212
McCandless, David, 116–17
McGonigal, Kelly, 49
McKean, Erin, 77–78
McRae, Lucy, 119
Meade, Alexa, 163
meaning
    conveying, 30–31
    in voice, 200–205
Mehrabian, Albert, 19
memorization process, 136–39, 150.
        See also scripted talks
mental preparation, 183–88
metaphors
    explanatory, 73, 75, 76, 77–78
    parable, 70–71
    persuasion priming, 88–90
Meyer, Pamela, 138, 144–45
Milk, Chris, 107
Mistry, Pranav, 102
Monbiot, George, 200–201
monitors, confidence, 193–95
morality, 41, 95, 96, 174, 249–51
motivation, 15–16, 185, 188, 244–45
Mullins, Aimee, 230
Murphy, Robin, 33
music, 215–16, 222
Musk, Elon, 5–6, 213–14

Nagy, Ricky and Gloria, 233
narration
  ancient roots of, x–xi, 63–64
  benefits of, 67
  closing with symmetry of, 173
  for connection, 59–61
  core elements of, 65
  of detective story, 92–93
  of dreams of future, 105–7, 172
  editing and context, 65–68
  effective, 59–60, 65–66, 68–70
  ineffective, 60–61, 66, 67
  of parables, 70–71
  for persuasion, 88–89
  true or fabricated, 68
Nasser, Latif, 216
Negroponte, Nicholas, 37, 190
nervousness
  as asset, 4–5, 51, 183, 188
  backup plan for, 187, 191
  in body language, 207
  fear response and, 3, 183
  management, 144, 183–88
  scripting and, 130–31, 133, 144, 191
99% Invisible, 212
Norris, Woody, 212
notes
  backup, 187, 191
  on cards, 192–93
  on confidence monitors, 193–95
  on hands, 197
  on lecterns, 189, 196–97
  on smartphones or tablets, 193
  on teleprompters, 195–96
  for unscripted talk, 143
Novogratz, Jacqueline, 4–5
Nuland, Sherwin, 51–52
Nyad, Diana, 171–72

Obama, Barack, 196
Oliver, Jamie, 158

opening
  acknowledgments at, 156–57
  curiosity, 160–63
  dramatic, 157–60
  teaser, 165–67
  visual, 163–65
OpenTED, 246
oration, 204–5
org bore, 25–26, 123
Oster, Emily, 93, 163
Oxman, Neri, 211

pacing
  movement, 206–7
  voice, 151, 203–5
Pallotta, Dan, 91, 92, 95
Palmer, Amanda, 36–37, 144, 173, 182
panoramic screens, 211
parables, 70–71
paradox of choice, 88, 89–90
passion, 202, 231
PechaKucha, 219
Perel, Esther, 173
persuasion. See also reason
  assumption demolition for, 86–87, 88
  narration for, 88–89
  priming for, 89–90
philosopher's secret, 247
photo credits, 122–23
Pierson, Rita, 172
Pink, Dan, 57–58, 208
Pinker, Steven, 78–79, 86–87, 96, 98
podcasting, live, 212–13
podiums, 189–91, 196–97
poetry, 214–15
politics, 61–62, 196, 250
Pop Up Magazine, 216
power posing, 170, 185
preparation. See also rehearsing;
    visual design
  backup, 187, 191

mental, 183–88
motivation for, 15–16, 185, 188,
     244–45
of scripted talks, 134–41
time limit, 34, 144, 154–55
under-, 24–25, 30, 141, 152, 169
of unscripted talks, 141–43, 146
wardrobe, 179–82
presentation design. *See specific
     formats*; visual design
presentation literacy, xii, 10, 245–46
priming, 89–90
Pritchard, Michael, 104
prompts. *See also* notes
teleprompter, 195–96
visuals as, 142–43, 192, 213–14
props, 210–11
psychosocial phenomena
ancient, x–xi, 63–64
creative genius, 88–89
empathy, 41, 64, 107, 250
experience simulation, 73–74
eye contact, 49
fear response, 3, 183
guarding, 47–48
happiness, 8, 72–76, 88–90, 247–48
impact bias, 74–75
laughter, 11, 54
listening, 18–19, 199–200
love, 29
paradox of choice, 88, 89–90
priming, 89–90
smiling, 49
tribal thinking, 61–62
public speaking
abuse of, 249–51
conversational vs., 10, 139–41, 152,
     203–5
fear of, 3, 183
formula for great, x, 12
human component of, 199, 249–50

Internet impact on, xi–xii, 221–23,
     238–45
lecture-style, 198
motivation for, 15–16, 185, 188, 244–45
as necessary skill, 227–28
oratory, 204–5
rhetoric, xii
as teachable skill, xii, 9–10

Raghava KK, 49
Ramachandran, V. S., 162
rambling, 24–25, 68, 144, 152
reading
listening vs., 198–201
from script, 132, 134, 136, 140, 189,
     194–96
reason
counter method of, 91–92
detective story for, 92–93
engagement tools, 94–95
if-then method of, 91
power of, 90–91, 95–96, 250–51
receptivity. *See* connection
reductio ad absurdum, 91–92
rehearsing
audience for, 149
feedback questions, 153–54
importance summary, 155
scripted talks, 136–39, 148–49
stage presence, 207
throughline testing, 42–43
time limits and, 154–55
unscripted talks, 147, 150–53
wardrobe, 181–82
Reid, Rob, 54–55
religion, 61–62, 250
reputation, 3, 23
revelation
categories of, 97
demonstrations, 102–4, 212
dreams of future, 105–7, 172

revelation (*cont.*)
  visuals for, 114–15
  wonder walks, 98–102, 118–19,
    163–64
rhetoric, xii
Rielly, Tom, 55–56, 115–16, 119
Rives, 138, 154–55
Roach, Mary, 99, 150, 208
Robbins, Tony, 221
Robinson, Ken, 40, 53, 69–70, 145–46,
  206
Ronson, Jon, 170–71, 215–16
Ronson, Mark, 143
Rosling, Hans, 83, 118, 222–23

Sacks, Oliver, 207
sales pitch, 22–24, 169
Sandel, Michael, 161–61
satire, 55, 56
Saunders, Ben, 69, 123
Schklair, Steve, 212
Schwartz, Barry, 32, 88, 89–90, 182
Schwartzberg, Louis, 101
Scott, Sophie, 11, 53
scripted talks
  improvisation with, 146–47
  language choice in, 139–40
  naturalness in, 130–31, 133, 136–39,
    141
  proponents of, 143–45
  pros and cons of, 134–35, 147
  reading, 132, 134, 136, 140, 189,
    194–96
  rehearsing, 136–39, 148–51
  strategies for, 135
  voice tips for, 201–2
self-interest, 36–37, 41, 57–59, 169,
  249–51. See also talk styles to
  avoid
Sense of Style, The (Pinker), 78–79
sensory stimulation, 211–12

Shirky, Clay, 150–51
Shirley, Stephanie, 207
silence, 101
simplification, 32, 36–37, 82, 115–16
simulation, 73–74, 107
Sirolli, Ernesto, 59–60
slide blizzard, 216–17, 219. *See also*
  visuals
smartphones, 157, 193
smiling, 49–50, 138
Smith, Clint, 215
Snowden, Edward, 221
Solomon, Andrew, 69, 140
Solomon, Susan, 149
soundtracks, 215–16
SpaceX, 5–6
Spielberg, Steven, 166
spoken word fusion, 214–15
stage presence
  body language for, 19, 206–7, 208
  nervousness and, 144, 183–88
  voice for, 198–205, 208
  wardrobe and, 179–82
stage setup. *See also specific formats*
  backup, 191
  confidence monitors in, 193–95
  glitches, 126, 180, 187
  lecterns in, 189–91, 196–97
  note cards in, 192–93
  smartphones and tablets in, 193
  teleprompters in, 195–96
standing ovation, 27
Stevenson, Bryan, 24, 54, 174
Stoetzel, Kelly, 179
Stoll, Clifford, 197, 207
Stone, Bill, 171
Stone, Mac, 128
Stone, Ruth, 88–89
StoryCorps, 109
storytelling. *See* narration
Strawson, P. F., 198

structure
   for demonstrations, 104
   for explanation, 79–80
   idea and throughline, 39–41
   for wonder walks, 99
surprise
   appearances, 220–21
   unexpectedness, 31–33, 74, 84,
      161–62
Sutherland, Rory, 146–47, 204
Sweeney, Julia, 130
synthetic happiness, 72–76

tablets, 193
talk delivery. *See* delivery
talk formats. *See also specific formats*;
      stage setup
   promise and peril of, 207, 223
talk styles to avoid
   inspiration performance, 26–29
   org bore, 25–26, 123
   ramble, 24–25, 68, 144, 152
   sales pitch, 22–24, 169
talk tools
   about, 43
   connection, 47–62
   explanation, 72–85
   mix and match, 109–10
   narration, 59–62, 63–71
   persuasion, 86–96
   revelation, 97–109
teaser opening, 165–67
technical considerations. *See* stage
      setup; visual design
technology
   age of knowledge and, 233–35
   Internet impact, xi–xii, 221–23,
      238–45
   talks on, 102–4, 107–8, 166, 212–13
   virtual audience, 222–23
   virtual presenters, 221–22

TED
   early development of, 228–29
   Ed Clubs, 245–46
   Fellows program, 239
   formation of, 228
   interconnective power of, 229–33,
      240–43
   Learning Wednesdays, 16
   mission of, xiii–xiv, 12, 238
   Open, 246
   rescue of, 6–8, 12, 231–33
   rules, 34, 132–33, 181, 190, 229
   scope of, xii–xiii, 240–43
   TEDx, xiii, 245
teleprompters, 195–96
Tenembaum, Abigail, 42
Thinking, Fast and Slow (Kahneman),
      168
Thorp, Jer, 128
throughlines
   characteristics of, 32–34
   checklist, 42
   defining, 30
   development of, 31, 34, 39, 42–43
   for explanation, 79–80
   for heavy topics, 41
   openings and, 158
   powerful, 31–32
   structure and, 39–41
   testing, 42–43
   time limitations and, 34–35, 39
   topics vs., 34, 36
   for wonder walks, 99
Thys, Tierney, 20
time limitations
   overrunning, 142, 154
   preparation for, 34–35, 144,
      154–55
   right approach to, 35, 36–43
   TED rules on, 34, 229
   wrong approach to, 35–36

topics
    condensing, 35–36
    heavy, 41, 59–60, 93, 163
    narrowing down, 36–42
    throughlines vs., 34, 36
transitions, 124–25, 151, 204
Treasure, Julian, 201, 216
tribal thinking, 61–62
trust, 49–50. *See also* connection
Turere, Richard, 9–10
Turin, Luca, 212
typefaces, 120–21, 122

Uncanny Valley, 137–38, 147, 152, 194
understanding
    cognitive load and, 115–16
    defining, 77
    explanation for, 77–81, 100, 115–16
    knowledge vs., 231–32
    pacing for, 203–4
unscripted talks
    advantages of, 134–35, 141
    disadvantages of, 144–45
    interviews, 213–14
    notes for, 143
    pitfalls, 142, 152
    proponents of, 145–46
    rehearsing, 147, 150–53
    scripting with, 146–47
    unprepared compared to, 24–25,
        141
    visual prompts in, 142–43, 192, 213–14

validation, third-party, 94–95
video
    design, 123–24, 125
    online, impact of, xi–xii, 240–45
    poetry, 215
virtual audience, 222–23
virtual presenters, 221–22
virtual reality, 107

visions of future, 105–9, 172, 234–35
visual design
    file transportation of, 125
    fonts and typefaces in, 120–21, 122
    legibility of, 121
    Lessig Method of, 216–17
    photo credits in, 122–23
    presentation software for, 119–20,
        126
    professionals, 126–27, 128
    rights and licensing for, 125
    testing, 125–26
    transitions in, 124–25
    version control of, 127–28
    for video, 123–24, 126
visuals
    art, 98, 99–100, 118–19, 163–64,
        219–20
    bad, 117, 122, 123
    blizzard, 216–17, 219
    on confidence monitors, 193–95
    to delight, 98–102, 118–19, 163–64
    for demonstration, 102–4, 212
    for explanation, 115–18, 122
    interviews with, 213–14
    live exhibition, 219–20
    necessity of, 113–14
    as opening hook, 163–65
    panoramic, 211
    as prompts, 142–43, 192, 213–14
    props as, 210–11
    for reasoning, 95
    for revelation, 114–15
    videopoetry, 215
    for visionary talks, 107–8
    for wonder walks, 98–102, 118–19,
        163–64
voice
    meaning in, 200–205
    oratory, 204–5
    pacing, 151, 203–5

reading or listening to, 198–201
scripted talk tips for, 201–2
spoken word, 214–15
variety in, 201–3
volume, 204–5
vulnerability, 50–53, 174, 186–87,
190

wardrobe, 179–82
Washington, Megan, 187
water, 104, 186
Watson, 234, 235
Whitacre, Eric, 222
Widder, Edith, 114, 166
Wiessner, Polly, 63–64

Wilson, Woodrow, 34–35
Woldhek, Siegfried, 92–93
wonder walks, 98–102, 118–19, 162–63
written word
    lyricism of, 136, 139–40, 174–75,
        214–15
    reading or listening to, 198–201
Wurman, Richard Saul, 6–7, 190,
    228–29, 231

Yong, Ed, 160
YouTube, 240–45

Zayid, Maysoon, 158
Zimmer, Carl, 164